Int
the Qur'an

Also available from Continuum:

Sacred Scriptures of the World Religions, Joan Price

Interpreting the Qur'an

A Guide for the Uninitiated

Clinton Bennett

continuum

Continuum
Continuum International Publishing Group
The Tower Building   80 Maiden Lane
11 York Road   Suite 704
London SE1 7NX   New York
                                       NY 10038

British Library Cataloguing-in-Publication Data
A catalogue record for this book is available from the British Library.

ISBN 10: HB: 0826499430
        PB: 0826499449
ISBN 13: HB: 9780826499431
        PB: 9780826499448

Library of Congress Cataloging-in-Publication Data

Bennett, Clinton.
  Interpreting the Qur'an : a guide for the uninitiated / Clinton Bennett.
    p. cm.
  Includes bibliographical references and index.
  ISBN-13: 978-0-8264-9943-1 (HB)
  ISBN-13: 978-0-8264-9944-8 (pbk.)
  ISBN-10: 0-8264-9943-0 (HB)
  ISBN-10: 0-8264-9944-9 (pbk.)
    1. Koran–Introductions. 2. Koran–Criticism, interpretation, etc. 3. Koran–
Paraphrases, English. I. Title.

BP130.B42 2009
297.1'2261–dc22

                                                                        2009010922

Typeset by Fakenham Photosetting Limited, Fakenham, Norfolk
Printed and bound in Great Britain by CPI Antony Rowe, Chippenham, Wiltshire

To

David Kerr D.Phil. (Oxon) (1945–2008)

Islamicist and Arabist, scholar of Christian–Muslim Relations and of Non-Western Christianity, my teacher and mentor.

His life and work was dedicated to the *humanum*, to the cause of human solidarity. With deep appreciation, I dedicate this book to his memory.

Contents

Acknowledgements

First, I want to acknowledge all those who over the years contributed to my understanding and appreciation of the Qur'an. My indebtedness to the work of others is reflected in references to their writing. I also wish to thank Continuum for commissioning this book. I am especially grateful to Rebecca Vaughan-Williams, my previous editor, to Kirsty Schaper, my current editor, to Tom Crick, Humanities Assistant and to Ryan Masteller, Production Editor for working with me on this and on other projects. My wife, Rekha Sraker Bennett and our son, George of course merit mention for encouragement and unstinting support. Research for this book was carried out in the Sojourner Truth Library of the State university of New York at New Paltz as well as on the World Wide Web. Images reproduced in the concluding chapter were copied from Wikipedia: the first, an eleventh century Qur'an from the article "Qur'an"; the second, a bismillahi from the article on "Isdlamic Calligraphy"; the third, an eleventh century example of the kufic script from the article on "Kufic". All three images are in the Public Domain.

I consider it a privilege to be able to write a book on the Qur'an. I sincerely hope that no offence is given by what I have written. My aim is to elucidate, de-perplex and illuminate, but also to help strangers to the Book, the uninitiated, to begin to develop an appreciation for, even a love of, the Qur'an. Some of my own favourites are: lightning and thunder blazing God's praise (13: 13); The metaphor that if the oceans were ink they would dry up before exhausting God's word (18: 109; 31: 27) and the recurring invitation to travel the world and sail the seas to reflect on and remember God's bounty. As an author, I love reference to God teaching by "the pen" (96: 4). I realized as I paraphrased the many warnings about Judgement and descriptions of the fires of hell that this is a major theme, from which there is literally no escape unless we turn to God. Yet the Qur'an is finely balanced; the threat of hell is always accompanied by the possibility and promise of paradise. References to Satan exactly match those to Angels. God's mercy, which the opening declaration of 113 out of 114 chapters announces, permeates the whole Book. Nor should we interpret physical depictions too literally; the Qur'an uses allegory and metaphor to communicate its message.

While working on this project, my masters' and doctoral mentor, Professor David Kerr, passed away. David was Director of the Centre for the Study of Islam and Christian–Muslim Relations, Birmingham, when I began my research. When I was first enrolled at the Centre, it was a new enterprise; it has been described as among the great academic ventures of the twentieth century ("Professor David Kerr", *The Times*, 5 June 2008, citing a Muslim scholar; www.timesonline.co.uk/tol/comment/obituaries/article4068574.ece). David later moved to the Hartford Seminary, Connecticut, followed by the University of Edinburgh. Finally, he was chair in missiology at Lund, Sweden. David was one of two men who taught me Arabic: although my linguistic achievements and ability are very modest, I remain hugely in his debt; the other teacher was a native speaker. Although another supervisor took over directing my studies when David went to Hartford, he continued to mentor me on visits to the UK. In 1989 my first trip ever to the USA was for a final consultation with David before submitting my Ph.D. thesis that December. David's consuming passion was promoting human solidarity. He wanted to penetrate through bias and prejudice to the true heart of the cultural and religious Other, whom we too often demonize.

Never once in those exciting, almost pioneer days at Selly Oak, when we seemed to be engaged in a new approach to Muslims, did David even hint that the subject of the Qur'an might not be "our" God as well. His love for the unspeakable eloquence of the Qur'an communicated itself through the passages he chose to teach. One of the earliest passages we learned by heart was Surah 103, "By time, man is indeed in a state of loss, except for those who collaborate in righteous acts, persevere in patience and never abandon Truth." We sat in the late, dark afternoon in the old Library, sometimes as snow fell outside, reciting this rhythmic, beautiful passage with heart-felt conviction even as David corrected our errors. Here we have the universal, open message that is central to the whole Book; God wants us to cooperate, to break down the walls that separate us, to join hands in combating injustice, oppression and exploitation. God wants us to build a world of peace and prosperity for all people. As a Christian, I am aware that readers of this book and of the Qur'an who share my faith will go away with some unanswered questions. I hope, though, that readers will cease asking one question, "Are Islam and Christianity incompatible, destined to remain mutually hostile?" I hope that, regardless of unresolved issues about Jesus' status and Christian claims, readers will agree with me that the Qur'an invites Christian–Muslim cooperation to make the world a better place. I am convinced that when we find ourselves between the devil and a hard place, God prefers us to join hands against evil than to argue about "unity", "trinity" and other issues. God, says the Qur'an, will ultimately decide such disputes between us; meanwhile let's compete in good works (5: 48), never abandoning Truth, always persevering against the odds we face, against those who want to divide the world into "us" and "them", "haves" and "have-nots". What follows, inadequate as it is, is dedicated to David's memory and remembrance.

Clinton Bennett
SUNY New Paltz
NY USA

Introduction: The Qur'an, The Prophet and the Community

The role of religion in society, whether it is "good" or "bad", is currently a topic of intense interest, generating books from a range of perspectives on both sides of the debate. Some in the West regard Islam as especially problematic, so much so that the words "terrorism" and Islam have become all but synonymous. Many buy "translations" of the Qur'an to find out what the Book actually says, why Muslims do what they do and believe what they believe. Are Muslim acts or beliefs, people ask, consistent with what the Book says? Farid Esack (2005) comments that while post-9/11 sales of copies of translations of the Qur'an have rocketed, he doubts if few will read more than a few pages, since "the Qur'an is a difficult book for strangers ... and for many Muslims ... to negotiate" (191). Rana Kabbani (1989) says that she firmly believes that the book cannot be translated, that non-Arabic speakers who read the Qur'an in translation, Muslim or non-Muslim, "are simply not reading the same book" (98). Kabbani is a long way off being a conservative or a traditional Muslim, so her comments represent a pessimistic opinion about non-Muslim ability even to read, let alone to comprehend, the Qur'an. Traditionally, a rendering of the Qur'an into another language is regarded as an "interpretation" and, as such, is a type of *tafsir*. *Tafsir*, which means interpretation (from *fassara*, to explain) is the science of Qur'anic exegesis. The word used for a translation, *tarjuman*, also implies "interpretation"; someone who translates Arabic into another language must also explain what they translate. A translation that also elucidates meaning does not necessarily render a word in one language with a single word in another. Sometimes, a whole phrase is needed for the sake of clarity.

The view that the Qur'an is the Qur'an only when read in Arabic is not merely because of issues involved in translation. Rather, the Qur'an is conscious of its own Arabic identity; see for example 12: 2; 13: 37; 16: 103. At least 11 verses refer to the Qur'an as a "revelation" in Arabic. Muslims believe that the language of the Qur'an is inimitable, unrivalled in Arabic literature. God chose Arabic because of the beauty, expressiveness, clarity and eloquence of the language. Yet the Qur'an is equally aware of the universal nature of its message. As a book whose message is intended for the whole world, that message must be communicated to non-Arabic speakers. Despite some reservations about the adequacy of any rendering into another language, the task of translation took place during Muhammad's life. When he sent some companions to seek asylum in Ethiopia, they took with them a written record of Surah 19, which was read in an Amharic translation to the Negus. Salman al-Farsi, who became a Muslim during the event of the *hijrah*, rendered portions of the Qur'an into Persian. The jurist Abu Hanifa allowed Muslims who had not yet learned Arabic to pray and also to "recite and memorize the Qur'an" in another language because "this is better than abandoning it altogether" (cited by Saeed 2008, 121).

In its original Arabic, the Qur'an, when read or recited, makes an eloquent and beautiful sound. In sharp contrast, translations tend to be clumsy and sometimes almost incoherent. The latter is a far cry from what Muslims believe to be a book of unrivalled literary merit, because its origin is divine. The science of Qur'anic recitation, *tajwid*, which means "make beautiful" is sophisticated and complex. Famous reciters have been compared with opera singers in the Western world, or perhaps with rock stars. The Qur'an was written in what technically can be called rhymed prose or *Saj'*. This is especially true of the shorter chapters. Much use is also made of assonance, as well as rhyme and of what Sells calls "nasalization". Sells describes some chapters as having a hymn-like quality (Sells, 16). He also draws attention to use of alliteration and of what he describes as a "staccato rhythm" (53). In some passages, this builds up rapidly to a dramatic change of voice, for example, from one of warning into a sad, plaintive lament. Chapter 82 is an excellent example of all these linguistic features; there is "staccato assonance based on consonants and short vowels (*fatarat, intatharat, fujjirat, bu'thirat, akhkharat*)" followed by longer vowels that give "a softening and deepening effect" shifting voice (at verse 6) to a "lament" that contrasts sharply with the "roughness of the earlier verses and their evocation of the apocalypse" (Sells, 176).

Saj', says Neuwirth, "is a particularly succinct rhythmic diction where single phrases are marked off by prose-rhyme, *fasila*". "This pattern", she continues, "of phonetic correspondence between the verse endings is not only looser than poetry ... but also more flexible, thus allowing for semantically related verses to be bracketed by a rhyme of their own and clearly distinct groups to be marked off" (Neuwirth, 98). Attempting in translation to do justice to the literary power of the original is always a challenge. The words that begin every *surah* except Surah 9, *bismillah arahman arahim*, give us one example of resonance. Translating the meaning of this simple Arabic sentence, too, illustrates the challenge involved. *Rahman* and *rahim* share the root, *rhm*, with the meaning of "mercy". Every Arabic word is built up from a base-word consisting of three consonants; vowels and prefixes are added. Muhammad, for example, is from *hmd*, which means "blessed". Islam is from *slm*, with the root meaning of "peace", as in *salam*. *Rahim* as "mercy" is widely used. *Rahman* denotes that "being merciful" is intrinsic to God's nature. It refers to God's "*rahmaniyya*" (Sherif, 26), to God as a "reservoir of Compassion" (Lawrence, 198). Used exclusively of Allah, *Rahman* is also one of God's Names. Pickthall rendered the phrase, "In the Name of Allah, the Beneficent, the Merciful". Ali chose "Most Gracious, Most Merciful". One possibility to convey the meaning and the distinction between the two Arabic words is "The Merciful Lord of Mercy". Sells, attempting to retain assonance, chose "the Compassionate, the Caring" (Sells, 21). Lawrence chose "Full of Compassion, ever Compassionate". Yet here we have five English words where two serve in Arabic. Although "mercy" and "compassion" are similar, the root of both *rahman* and rahim is usually rendered as "mercy", not compassion. Haleem comments that rendering the Arabic as, for example, "Compassionate and Merciful" using "two words with different roots" loses what he calls "the connection" between the two original words (Haleem, 16). Sells' preference for "compassionate" and "caring" gives us two words, but words that have different roots. Lawrence explains his rendering: "To my ear" he says "the use of two dependent qualifiers seems closer to the Qur'anic tone than using a noun and an adjective from the same root" (Lawrence, 198). As imperfect as a translation or paraphrase may be, I agree with Sells that the "impossibility of perfect translation" does not mean it is "futile" to try. The effort to do so "is an essential element of human experience" (Sells, 22). Some argue that an "approximation of meaning" may be the best we can hope for from any translation, although I find this too pessimistic about the possibility of genuine cross-linguistic and cross-cultural understanding. This would place the goal of a peaceful, unified world out of reach. "Muslims", says Sultan, "feel that the translation process creates meanings that were never intended in the original Scripture" (Sultan 2004, 32). He points out that some translations "are extremely inaccurate and even damaging to the Koran's message" (57).

Similarly, Ali says that translations by "non-Muslim and anti-Muslim" writers have caused a great deal of "mischief" (Ali, xx). Yet, says Sultan, "for those who do not read Arabic, translations of the Koran allow them to begin to understand the distinctive ideas in the book" (2004, 86).

One translation issue is that the Arabic script does not use punctuation, which raises issues about where sentences begin and end. Esack illustrates this with a passage that has considerable relevance to the whole business of understanding and interpreting the Qur'an, Surah 3: 7. Referring to the "allegorical" verses of the Qur'an, the passage can be read as "None save God and those whose hearts are rooted in knowledge know their exact meaning" or as "None but God knows its final meaning." Depending on where the "ayah stops" 3: 7 can be used to justify the claim that some people possess a special hermeneutical authority or that the Qur'an contains mysteries that none of us can grasp, which remind us that God is greater and more knowledgeable than we are (Esack 2005, 58). Sells comments that some of the early chapters are actually at their most powerful when "the exact relationship of one statement to another hangs in the balance and, instead of freezing into some clearly definable meaning, continues to resonate and pose questions that only a lifetime of searching can answer" (Sells, 27).

The non-Muslim's tendency to try to read the Qur'an from start to finish can lead to perplexity. Read in this way, the content appears disjointed; the book is not a continuous narrative, and different types of material dealing with a range of topics are found in the same chapter. Non-Muslims and Muslims both comment on the challenge to understanding posed by the order of the Qur'an's chapter for the uninitiated, that is, for those who are unfamiliar with the way the Muslims read, use and interpret the book. Some Muslims regard the fact that the book is different from other books as evidence of its inimitability; *different* from other books, it should not be treated, or read, in the same way. Sarwar and Toropov suggest that many misunderstanding arise "about Islam by non-Muslims from the assumption" that the Qur'an is "equivalent to the Judeo-Christian Bible, or to the Hindu Bhagavad-Gita" or to "other religious texts". On the contrary, they say, "the Qur'an is set apart from these texts ... and, in fact, from all the literature found on earth" (xix). The order of chapters does not follow a chronology of, for example, the story of the life of Muhammad and that of the early Muslim community. Material is often repeated, while the voice switches from addressing one audience to another. Critics describe the content as jumbled and confused. "Experiencing the Koran", write Sarwar and Toropov, "has been compared to navigating a wild river" which "swirls and twists and turns, then doubles back from where it came ... and then, just when one thinks one knows where the river is going, it curves again in an entirely new direction" (63). Esack comments that "because the Qur'an is the recited word in addition to being the written word, this seeming disjuncture is of little consequence to most Muslims". "Repetitions", he writes, "are seen as God's repeated reminders, legal texts in the middle of a narrative as God drawing our attention to what has to be learnt from the text, breaks in a narrative reflects God's freedom from literary patterns or suggest that the information contained therein is often incidental, while the mode, sound patterns and inner rhythm are central" (Esack 2005, 66). See Q39: 23 on the purpose of repetition, of which the Qur'an was self-conscious.

As officially arranged, with the exception of Chapter 1, which serves a liturgical function, the chapters are ordered roughly according to size, from longer to shorter. There is a chronological aspect, though, because chapters are identified as having originated in Mecca (early), or in Medina (later). Some verses in a chapter designated as Meccan may have been revealed at Medina or vice versa. The designation rests on the provenance of the opening verses. Normally, Muslims read those chapters or verses of the Book which are appropriate to the particularity of the moment; for example, passages about death and the hereafter at a funeral, comforting passages when someone is unwell, The book, too, was intended to be *heard* rather than *read* – it is quintessentially meant to be an *aural experience*. Muslims, incidentally, often dislike use of the term *text* to describe the Qur'an, which reduces it to the status of any other humanly constructed discourse. On the other hand, the Qur'an is also self-aware of its existence as a written record, as well as of its orality. It refers to use of the pen, describes itself as a *Kitab* (Book) and speaks of having been inscribed, or sent down from the "mother of the book" (43: 4) and from a "heavenly table" (57: 22)

We know that portions had been written down by scribes before the conversion of Umar (615–16) at least five or six years before the *hijrah* (622, migration from Mecca to Medina). There are occasions when the whole book is read from start to finish. During the month of Ramadan, when the first revelation came to Muhammad, it is recited over cycles of three days. Those known as *hafiz* learn the whole book by heart. From the time of the earliest complete editions of the Qur'an, it has been read and studied as a whole. The difference, though, between a Muslim and a non-Muslim picking up and reading the book cover to cover is familiarity with its content, which the former has acquired, by frequently hearing and reading portions non-sequentially. Sells puts it like this, "The Qur'anic experience is not the experience of reading a written text from beginning to end." "Rather", he says, "the themes, stories, hymns and laws of the Qur'an are woven through the life stages of the individual" as well as through the "key moments of the community" (12).

Given the difficulty of reading the Qur'an with understanding, many non-Muslims who believe they have acquired a sympathetic appreciation of the Book have attempted to help others do the same. These include Kenneth Cragg (1994 and 2005), Neal Robinson (2003) and Richard Drummond (2005). These books discuss how Muslims understand the process by which Muhammad received the Qur'an, and how it was subsequently ordered, and attempt to illuminate the content of the Qur'an, exploring its teachings, the historical context, the 'text' in the context of Muhammad's life and Muhammad's experience of revelation. Some also discuss how non-Muslims have deconstructed the text, based on the supposition that it is a human composition. Robinson, who became a Muslim since writing the first edition of his book, writes about the morphology of the Qur'an as he examines the structure of the Arabic and anchors the Book in 'space and time'. In addition to these and other books by non-Muslims, Muslim writers such as Farid Esack (2005) and Rafiq Zakaria (1991) have also been written primarily to help non-Muslims gain an appreciation of the Book. Zakaria's approach is somewhat different. He begins by locating the Qur'an within the prophet's biography, then offers his own translation or "interpretation" of a selection of chapters. Personally, I highly recommend Abdullah Saeed's 2006 and 2008 books for erudition, clarity and for what I regard as a progressive approach. Two attempts, *The Koran for Dummies* (Sultan 2004) and *The Complete Idiot's Guide to the Koran* (Sarwar and Toropov 2003) are especially interesting, since they target a more popular readership. Written in an easy-to-understand style, they cover the same material as the more academic texts but also serve to introduce Islam as practised by Muslims. Aware that non-Muslims often view Islam as oppressive of women, as violent and even as anti-intellectual, both texts specifically discuss these issues. This suggests that writing about the Qur'an cannot easily avoid being apologetic. Esack says that post-9/11, the idea that the Qur'an sanctions violence has become popular. He offers an alternative understanding of the "text". I have not alluded to those who write on the Qur'an or about Muhammad from a polemical stance. A recent example here is Robert Spencer's *The Truth About Muhammad: Founder of the World's Most Intolerant Religion* (2006).

Is there scope for yet another introduction to the Qur'an? Arguably, a non-Muslim reader who sits down with a copy of the Qur'an and allows their reading to be guided by any of the above texts is likely to make more progress in appreciation and understanding than if they only read the Qur'an itself. However, what none of the above texts attempt is a summary or paraphrase of the whole of the Qur'an at the same time as locating the chapters within the story of early Islam as told in such historical texts as the *sira* (biographies) and *hadith* (sayings of Muhammad). What follows in this book, by a non-Muslim scholar of Islam who has wrestled with the Qur'an for almost 30 years, offers a brief summary of content within a framework that allows discussion of both the meaning or interpretation of the verses and their application in Muslim practice. Aware of problems associated with approach, I use, as far as this is possible, the order of the chapters in which they were probably originally revealed to Muhammad, which is different from the order of the standard Qur'an. This approach takes seriously Muslim conviction that the Qur'an has to be understood in the light of Muhammad's life. By utilizing Muhammad's life itself, and the developing story of the Muslim community, this approach untangles and de-perplexes the seemingly unconnected content of the Qur'an, weaving its chapters and verses into a continuous narrative. The relationship between book, messenger and community is taken to be of central concern in any attempt to understand the meaning and message of the Qur'an. On the one hand, what follows appreciates how Muslims revere the content of the Qur'an and tends to affirm a traditional, or standard, account. On the other hand, it does not avoid problematical readings that cannot be ignored but which can be revisited and reinterpreted. This book is therefore also a critical account. There is no reason why a traditional interpretation, even one that many Muslims assume to be correct, must be accepted without question. Some Muslims may challenge this on the basis of Muhammad's saying, "My community will not agree in error", that is, that if consensus exists on an issue, it represents the legitimate Islamic position. Others may point to the existence of a variety of opinion of various matters, and cite the saying that "difference of opinion is mercy" for the community. It is certainly the case that Muslims in every generation revisit the content of the Qur'an as they seek guidance for new circumstances, which the message of the Qur'an needs to address. Others stress that while, for Muslims, the Qur'an is divine, the interpretive task is human and can never claim to be other than provisional.

What people take as a consensus or even as the "right" interpretation has probably never been tested; the majority of Muslims have not expressed their thoughts on the issue. Dominated by religiously trained male scholars called 'ulema (from 'ilm, knowledge; singular *alim*), women's voices have rarely, in the past, contributed to interpretation. Esack and Saeed support the democratization of Qur'anic interpretation. When a group of untrained Muslims formed their own study circle in South Africa, they attracted the "ire of the 'ulema who, fearful of the loss of power entailed once their own position as gatekeepers to the text were forfeited, warned that the lay students of the Qur'an, would 'get lost.'" They argued "that 'it is not possible for a layman to study the Quran ... without the guidance of a qualified *Ustaz* (teacher) and that ... such study paves the path to *jahannam* (hell)'" (Esack 2005, 25–6). Saeed similarly writes of how more and more Muslims who have not attended religious schools are "attempting to read and understand the Qur'an for themselves." "All Muslims", he says, "have an equal right to understand the Scriptures according to their ability and skills" and, whether "the text is read in Arabic or in translation, aiming at some understanding of God's word is not a sin; on the contrary it reflects obedience to the Qur'anic command to think and reflect on its meaning" (Saeed 2006, 22).

Order of Revelation

There is no universal agreement on the order of revelation, which does raise problems for the approach I am adopting. Some verses of chapters were revealed at different times, while some Muslims contend that certain later verses cancel certain earlier verses, which also interrupts the order of revelation. The quest for the original order of the Qur'an, or for the order of revelation, too, became associated with Orientalist scholarship of the Qur'an that also deconstructed the text, tracing content to pre-existing sources. The idea that the Qur'an was composed or compiled by Muhammad, and not revealed to him by God, offends Muslims. Although Muslims, including some of the earliest and most reputable commentators on the Qur'an, have reconstructed the original order of revelation, this did not become a major concern, since the canonical order is believed to be itself the result of divine oversight. Jones (2001) comments that the "standard order appears to have been drawn up precisely to avoid questions of chronology" (xx).

Non-Muslim scholarship has posited linguistic development over time, suggesting that either the writer matured as an author, or materials from different, composite sources were gathered together. While God may speak with a different "voice" to different audiences, the idea that an analysis of linguistic style can identify when chapters were "written" is anathema to Muslims. Esack writes of how the Qur'an "and its language came to be viewed as timeless ... independent of any 'non-divine' elements". Thus, it "cannot be subjected to any linguistic principles" (Esack 2005, 69). Traditionally, while Muslims do locate verses within the "situation of revelation" (asbub-al-nuzul) to help illuminate their meaning and context, they also argue that some chapters do not require knowledge of the original context. Their content, they say, is unrelated to particular circumstances and makes clear sense without contextualization. Importantly, however, only material believed to be of universal application can become the basis of law. This is a subtle distinction, since material of universal application may have been revealed in response to a particular circumstance. The issue is whether the material in question was intended exclusively for that specific moment, or for all moments.

Esack says that while the situations of revelation play a significant role in *tafsir*, there has also been a certain reluctance to pursue this approach too far, lest Muslims convey the impression that context somehow dictated content (1997, 102) or compromises the "ontological otherness of the Quran" (2005, 125). Also, he says, acknowledgement that much of the *hadith* literature on which "all the *asbab* accounts are based" is unreliable raises serious questions about authenticity. Saeed says that on the one hand the ability of these accounts to "provide an understanding of the actual socio-historical context is limited" while on the other hand "as far as a significant number of verses of the Qur'an are concerned it is difficult to understand the meaning properly without a basic understanding of the context in which they were revealed" (2008, 2).

The earliest attempt to reconstruct the original order of revelation was by Ibn 'Abbas (died 687), a cousin of Muhammad and one of the earliest and most renowned exegetes, known as *tarjuman-al-Quran* (interpreter of the Qur'an). Many subsequent Muslim sequences were derived from Ibn Abbas' pioneer work. Later scholars also had access to the collections of *hadith* that had not been compiled at the time. In choosing a sequence to follow, I opted for Badruddin Zarkashi's. Zarkash (died 1390) also attempted an explanation of the standard order, which involved four rules. First, chapters beginning with *h-m* (cryptic or disjointed letters) all follow each other. Second, many chapters are linked at the end and beginning by their content or meaning. Third, some chapters in sequence have a common end rhyming pattern. Fourth, there is a resemblance between the rhyming patterns of "entire chapters clustered together" (Esack 2005, 65). As we shall see, Zarkash's labours have impacted feminist scholarship; he edited a collection of *hadith* narrated by Aisha, Muhammad's wife.

Appendix 1 compares the sequences of Ibn 'Abbas, Zarkashi, Nöldeke and Rodwell. Theodor Nöldeke (1836–1930) pioneered Western scholarship in this area, so much so that most "Western students of the text have until recently remained largely beholden to Nöldeke's reconstruction" (Donner, 33). His prize-winning *Geschichte des Korans* appeared in 1859. John M. Rodwell (1808–1900), whose translation of the Qur'an was published in 1861, drew heavily on the sequence developed by Gustav Weil (1808–89) in his *Mohammed, der Prophet* (1843). Jones comments that Nöldeke's sequence was also "heavily dependent" on the "traditional Muslim dating" and cannot be said to represent a "real advance" (xx). My comparison shows that all agree on 96 as the first revelation, while the Muslims and non-Muslims part company on the second, with the Muslims opting for 68, the non-Muslims for 74. However, all include 74 in their first five. The non-Muslims Nöldeke and Rodwell list 68 at 18 and 17 respectively. There is general agreement on the order of the earlier passages, less agreement on the last Meccan chapter. The possibilities are 8, 29 (Muslim) and 34 (non-Muslim). According to Denffer, 23 is another possibility (Denffer, 87). Zarkash lists 8 as the second Madinah passage; the two non-Muslims locate 29 four places earlier but 8 as ten later. Denffer, whose book I used for Zarkash's sequence, omits 1 from the order, commenting that some identify this as Meccan, some as Medinan. For this reason, I place it at 114 under Zarkash's sequence. A few scholars identify this as the first. There is, across the board of possible sequences, less agreement about which is the last passage of all; possibilities are 114, 47 and 5. Denffer mentions 2: 281; 2: 282; and 2: 278 as possibilities (Denffer, 28). Ali says that 5: 3 is probably the last "words of the Qur'an to be revealed" (1709). Esack lists 9: 128–9, 18: 110 and 110: 1–3 as "some of the verses suggested as the final revelation due to their poignancy and seemingly appropriateness in concluding the Qur'an" (2005, 53). Rodwell's translation reordered the chapters to follow his chosen sequence, which makes his approach and mine more or less identical. In claiming that my approach is "fresh" I openly acknowledge Rodwell, the work of Ibn 'Abbas, Zarkash and all those who have worked on reconstructing the order of revelation. Rodwell's brief annotations shed light on why he located some passages where he did, but he did not systematically comment on context.

In what follows, I do not attempt to relate every chapter to a specific context. Rather, I situate them against the background of events that took place around about the time they were probably first uttered by Muhammad. When there is good reason to depart from Zarkash, I explain why. When passages can be anchored in events with reasonable accuracy and confidence, this will be evident from the narrative. Jones goes so far as to say that this is only possible "with some of the Medinan surah" (xxi). I think we can locate many *surahs* against the backdrop of wider events with a reasonable degree of certainty. When we can confidently "relate *surahs* to events in Muhammad's life", as Jones puts it, there is sometimes so much information that only a summary can be attempted in what follows. No effort is therefore made to present the complete biography of Muhammad; that would require more words than my publisher allowed. Nor do I comment on every verse that merits discussion, since that would also require a lengthier treatment. Many Muslim commentaries run to multiple volumes. Also, I do not always identify verses in a chapter thought to have been revealed at a different time, except when this creates the need to deal with a passage elsewhere in the book. Appendix 2, however, indicates when verses in either Meccan or Medinan chapters are thought to belong to the other category.

In producing the paraphrase that forms the substance of this book, I have consulted a range of translations as well as the Arabic text. Paraphrasing avoids the need to try to replicate the rhythm and cadence of the original, although some attempt is made in this book to convey an impression of this important quality. Paraphrasing also means that what is offered is a digest, not a word-for-word rendering. Of necessity, this is considerably shorter than the original, so it is not meant to substitute for the Qur'an itself. The aim is to clarify, de-perplex and illuminate meaning. The first rendering of the Qur'an into Latin was also a paraphrase. Commissioned by Peter the Venerable (d. 1156), who "spurred the Christian initiative to understand, rather than vilify, Islam", this translation, although describing the Qur'an as the lies of a pseudo-prophet, yet engaged deeply both with the text and with what "Muslims themselves took the Qur'an to mean" (Lawrence, 101). Robert of Ketton, the principal translator, took the trouble to consult Muslims before offering "his own 'loose' translations of difficult words or complex passages". He drew on commentary to elucidate meaning, even if the result led to an expansion of the original passage (Lawrence, 103).

My own initial reading of sections of the Qur'an was through Arabic. I majored in world religions on my undergraduate degree at Manchester University, where at the time it was still called Comparative Religion. However,

I studied Indian and ancient Iranian religion. I neither learned anything about Islam nor read independently in that area. I hoped to work in India with the Baptist Missionary Society; I was training for ordination at the time. As it happened, my candidacy to the Society was successful but due to visa issues I was designated for service in Bangladesh, a majority Muslim country. Subsequently, I found myself turning to the study of Islam. Graduating from Manchester in 1978, I spent the next academic year attending the Centre for the Study of Islam and Christian–Muslim Relations at the Selly Oak Colleges, now part of Birmingham University. Arabic was an integral part of the programme, so I first heard and read the Qur'an in its original tongue. Instead of the clumsy, inelegant English of a translation, I listened to the beauty and rhythm of the Arabic. This seminal experience of the Qur'an coloured all my later engagement with the scripture with a love for the tone and sound of the Arabic language. Although much of my subsequent exploration of meaning draws on translations, when I encounter a rendering that can best be described as dull, or as prosaic, I remember with deep appreciation my earliest exposure to the book. While working on his acclaimed *The Koran Interpreted* (1955) during his tenure as head of Classics at Cairo University, Arthur John Arberry (1905–69) wrote of how the "thrilling rhythms of the Koran" came freshly alive for him when he sat on his verandah during Ramadan, listening to "the white-bearded Shaykh who chanted the Koran for the pious delectation of" his neighbour. Then, he returned to the task of interpretation with a deepened appreciation for the cadences and depth of the original, even when "the ancient commentators" differed "in their understanding of a word or phrase" and he was challenged with adjudicating between diverse opinions (28).

I am not a professional scholar of Arabic, so I do not claim to possess the expertise to undertake a complete translation. On the other hand, I know enough to check references in the original and even, when needed, to identify what I think is a better rendering, Luckily, there are enough existing efforts by people with undeniable skill to make the task of producing another translation redundant. Nonetheless, when passages appear in quotation marks they are my own somewhat free rendering unless sourced to a specified translation or within a quotation. For Arabic, I used the interlinear English and Arabic editions of Ali (2001) and Pickthall (1977). Some Muslims are of the view that only Muslims should translate the Qur'an. That, I suggest, would be risky, suggesting that the study of Islam has no place in the secular academy. Esack, who is as apt to cite a non-Muslim scholar whom he admires as he is a Muslim, speaks of how some non-Muslims are, if not "full citizens of the world of the Quran" neither "foreigners" nor "invaders" (2005, 7). I aspire to be what Esack calls "a friend of the lover", someone who has internalized "Muslim sensitivities" and writes about the Qur'an in a manner that begs the question, is he "actually in love with the Muslim's beloved?" (Esack 2005, 6). For convenience, I use the more common Mecca and Medina rather than Makkah and Madinah, except when citing. I use Qur'an, however, not Koran (except in citations) and Muhammad rather than Mohammad or other alternative renderings (again, unless citing). I use some diacritics. Convinced that my God and Allah are identical, I use the Arabic Allah and the English God interchangeably, sometimes in the same sentence.

The Qur'an: Muslim and Non-Muslim Approaches

Before outlining the content of this book, this Introduction sketches the standard Muslim view of the Qur'an and contrasts this with non-Muslim opinion. Discussion of non-Muslim opinion is not concerned with polemical attacks on the Qur'an but with serious scholarly investigation of its compilation and origins. This is essential background for any detailed analysis of the message of the Qur'an that aims to offer, on the one hand, what could be described as a faith-sensitive account while on the other hand also dealing with critical issues. Outsider scholarship is included because I am of the view that Religious Studies can not privilege insider-ship without running the risk of bias, of compromising its claim to objectivity and its place in the secular academy. Since I currently teach at a public university, this is pertinent! I also discuss how I intend to incorporate *tafsir* (Qur'anic exegesis) into this text in a way that I hope avoids raising too many questions for those unfamiliar with the genre. In outlining the sources used to create a synthesis between the *context* and the *content* of the Qur'an's 114 chapters, issues related to the historical reliability of the biographical and historical literature are discussed.

The Qur'an: The Muslim View

The Qur'an was revealed to the Prophet Muhammad over a period of 22 years, beginning towards the end of the month of Ramadan in the year 610

CE and ending shortly before his death in June 632 CE. Passages were "sent down" (*tanzil*) by God through the Angel of Revelation, Gabriel. When Muhammad received passages, he recited them, which he and his companions subsequently learned by heart. Some sources say that five or ten chapters would be memorized and studied at a time (Esack 2005, 80). Later, scribes were appointed who recorded passages on various writing materials, such as palm-leafs and scraps of wood. What was sent down was pre-recorded on the Heavenly Tablet. Revelation is the process of *wahy*, which in the Qur'an begins with Adam, the first prophet and ends with Muhammad, the final prophet. God also "reveals" instruction to the bees at 16: 68 and "inspires" Moses' mother with *wahy* at 28: 7. When revelation relates to women and men, its content has a strong moral bias, although there is also an "assumption that women, birds or angels cannot become messengers of God in the same way that men do" (Esack 2005, 42). Revelation is always from behind a veil, that is, it involves a heavenly mediator. The Qur'an is direct speech, speech in the first person. Muhammad is instructed to "speak" or to "recite". What he said was God's speech. More than 200 passages begin with "*qul*" (say) (Denffer, 78).

While what became standardized as 114 *Suwar*, anglicized as *surahs* (*surah* = something surrounded by a fence) was fixed by Gabriel during the 22-year period, the verses or *ayat* (anglicized as *ayahs*) (*ayah* = sign) were not always revealed at the same time. Due to the structure of Arabic, division into verses is less standardized; 6,228 is commonly cited. What has increasingly become the accepted verse division follows the Egyptian edition of 1923/4, used for example by Ali (2001). This omits as *ayahs* the opening *bismilah arahman ahrahim* with which 113 chapters begin. Muslims use a different division known as *ajza*, which was designed to facilitate recitation. There are 30 *ajza* of approximately the same length. A single section is a *juz*. During 632, Gabriel rehearsed the whole of the Qur'an with Muhammad. According to tradition, the standard order was "determined by the Prophet under the guidance of the Angel Gabriel in the year of his death" (Denffer, 68). By then, a complete written record may have existed. Under the third caliph, Uthman (644–56) an official *mushaf* (collection of *suhuf*, writing materials) was made. Zaid Ibn Thabit, a former scribe, supervised this process ensuring that only what could be authenticated was included. Other versions were then destroyed, which suggests that there may have been some differences. The name of each *surah* is often taken from a word that appears early in the chapter; some are named after the opening cryptic letters. A "large number ... have names related to a subject matter referred to in the *surah*" (Esack 2005, 61). We know from *hadith* that Muhammad called some chapters by their given names. Esack comments that Muslims either refer to the name of a chapter or say "the Qur'an says", then recite the passage without identifying this by name or by number.

Muslims believe not only that the process of authenticating the canon was faultless but that, unlike earlier scriptures which have become corrupt over time, the Qur'an self-protects from contamination; "the Arabic language is self-preserving" says Sultan, "the Koran strongly suggests that it is unchangeable and protects itself from corruption" (Sultan 2004, 56). The "Arabic" nature of the Qur'an, then, guarantees that it remains exactly as it was when Muhammad received it from God. Later, most Muslims came to believe in the uncreated, eternal Qur'an; as God's "word" (*Kalam*) it existed eternally until it was *sent down*. The gradual sending down is understood as necessary for several reasons; to strengthen Muhammad's heart, in response to circumstances, to make memorization easier and from consideration for Muhammad, since "revelation was a very difficult experience" (Denffer, 28–9). Muslim opinion on the Qur'an can be summarized as: it is word for word God's speech, containing no human elements; any similarity of content with another scripture or other material is either a happy coincidence or because that source was also revealed by God. Difference from similar content, such as a biblical story, means that the latter has been corrupted. The Qur'an corrects such deviations. When I compare Qur'anic and Bible stories in what follows, I am not implying that I regard the latter as the source of the former. Like Ali, my view is that such comparison illustrates meaning (xvii). However, the way in which the Qur'an frequently refers to these narratives, often in abbreviated form, strongly suggests that hearers were familiar with details and could easily supply these themselves. The Qur'an, too, is more interested in the moral message than in the details of these narratives, strongly suggested at 18: 22. The Topkapi Museum in Istanbul houses a manuscript of the Qur'an containing almost the entire content, dating from as early as late first, or early second century AH. Since reciting the Qur'an follows strict rules, printed editions often contain notations on when to pause, or when and how to lengthen a vowel. The art of correct recitation is *Tartil*.

Non-Muslim Opinion

Non-Muslim opinion tends to view the Qur'an as a more composite work. The assumption is that Muhammad drew on knowledge of Christian, Jewish and other stories, although he may not have had access to written sources. Non-Muslim scholarship of the Qur'an has involved tracing content to earlier sources and what can be described as reconstructing the "history of the Qur'an". Some non-Muslims accept that Muhammad was genuine and sincere; some depict him as a self-serving opportunist who made revelation up as he went along to advance his personal and political agenda. Designing an exotic, even erotic heaven he invented such legal provisions as allowing men four wives to attract converts. When he couldn't attract enough support by preaching he turned to conquest. Some non-Muslims accept that Muhammad was inspired by God, but find the idea that he contributed nothing to the Qur'an difficult to accept. Many non-Muslims assume that construction of a fixed text involved editing and redaction. In this view, the content of the Qur'an before June 632 and after the completion of Uthman's official version were almost certainly different.

Many non-Muslim scholars accept the traditional chronology, which dates Muhammad's birth at 570 CE, the beginning of revelation in 610, the *hijrah* in 622 and Muhammad's death in 632. Some think that later dates, such as 622 and 632 are more reliable, assuming that 570 for Muhammad's birth may be a retrogressive calculation to make him 40 when he received Surah 96. A few scholars have offered a radically different chronology, one that not only shifts the life of Muhammad forward but argues for a much longer period during which the Qur'an was compiled. Crone and Cook (1977) for example, regard the Meccan phase of Muhammad's career as a construction, a "recasting" (17) of his story, what German scholars call *Heilgeschichte*, salvation history (24–5). In addition, they think that that this *heilgeschichte* was constructed closer to the reign of caliph 'Abd al-Malik (d. 705) (18). The *hijrah* was not to Medina but from "Arabia into the conquered territories", specifically Palestine (9). The reconstruction drew explicitly on Jewish sources because it was linked with the conquest of Jerusalem, establishing a claim on the sacred city that trumped those of Jews and Christians. Similarly, Wansbrough (1977) challenged the standard account of the compilation and dating of the Qur'an, the traditional story of Muhammad's life and the process of "revelation". One reason why Wansbrough rejected the standard account was that, in his view, neither the style, structure or content of the received Qur'an suggests one source or its compilation over a short timescale. Instead, he posited multiple sources and a longer redaction process. He thinks there was a variety of material circulating, including some of Christian and Jewish – especially of Jewish – origin. In addition to his analysis that the Qur'an itself suggests multiple sources, he bases his argument on *tafsir* literature, which, in his view, rarely identifies the specific context of the passage on which it comments but rather creates an explanatory narrative (134). The "obvious source for most, if not all, of this material", he said, was "Rabbinical literature". What emerged as the Qur'an was subordinate to, rather than determinative of, the text of these commentaries (127). Stories were gathered from folklore, including biblical folklore, to flesh out a salvation history (135).

In addition to issues of chronology and sources, another issue that has preoccupied non-Muslims is the relationship between the Qur'an and pre-existing and contemporary poetry. Denial that Muhammad was a poet and that the Qur'an is poetry is a central Qur'anic motif. Muhammad's own hearers, however, saw similarity not only between the style of what he recited and the utterances of the *Kahini* (soothsayers, shamans) but also between how he and they "received" their "revelations". Many analysts see a correspondence between the rhymed prose style of the *Kahini* and the Qur'an, although some suggest significant distinguishing differences. Graham and Kermani, for example, describe the language of the Qur'an as "neither poetry nor rhyming prose" and cite poets whom "the people of Mecca consulted … on how technically to categorize Muhammad's recitations" as confirming that it "does not conform to any known genre of metrical language" (127). Others recount a story that the grand-daughter of the renowned pre-Islamic poet Imr al-Qais once declared that she had heard Surah 54 before, that indeed it had been composed by her grandfather (verses 1, 29, 31, 46 are found word for word in the 'Poem of al-Qais'; see Masood, 185). This similarity is simply a happy coincidence for Muslims, similar to a story about Umar. Listening to Muhammad reciting a passage, Umar exclaimed out loud as Muhammad was drawing to a close. Muhammad then responded that what Umar had just said was exactly what Gabriel had dictated as the ending of the revelation. For Umar, this evidenced his "affinity with Revelation". When a similar incident occurred involving the scribe bin Abi Sarh, he apostatized. Since he was not a prophet, Abi Sarh disbelieved that he could possibly be a recipient of revelation (Esack 2005, 82).

Non-Muslims also point out that the script used to record the Qur'an has evolved; there is a stylistic difference between the shorter passages and the later, longer ones. These have "little poetic shaping" and "strongly suggest an almost immediate fixation in writing" or they may "have been written compositions to begin with" (Neuwirth, 101). Leemhuis notes that the "Arabic script … distinguished only eighteen different characters, while the full alphabet has twenty-eight consonants" (146). On the one hand, this could indicate that the written manuscripts, set alongside a "strong tradition of oral recitation", were a type of "mnemonic device" to aid vocalization by those who "already knew" the text. On the other hand, "it opens up the possibility that the fully vocalized texts that were eventually prepared could have contained erroneous vocalizations, further clouding our perception of the relationship of today's vocalized text to the revelations of Muhammad's time – that is, of the relationship of the Qur'an, as we have it today, to its presumed historical context" (Donner, 32). The earliest manuscripts, which do not indicate vowels, have no "diacritical marks to distinguish two or more consonants that were written with the same shape" (Donner, 32). Early manuscripts separate *surahs* with a space; later, the titles appear in a "deliberately different calligraphic style" (Gilliot, 48).

Others, Muslims and non-Muslims, point out that if God chose Arabic because it was a straightforward language that hearers would find easy to comprehend, the language of the Qur'an must be related with the written and spoken language of seventh-century Arabia. Zaid (1998) and Esack (2005) stress that the Qur'an was communicated to Muhammad in a language that both he and his audience understood. Since it set out to convey a clear, comprehensible message, "the message of Islam could not have had any effect if the people who first received it could not have understood it; they must have understood it within their socio-cultural context" (Zaid, 200). Esack stresses that while majority Muslim opinion insists on the eternal, timeless and divine nature of the Qur'an, which, as "God's speech … cannot be subjected to any linguistic principles", the "problem of God's speech of necessity having to coincide with human speech for effect and meaning remains" (2005, 69). Thus, he says, "we need to win the text back as an Arabic text – and Arabic is an historical language, part of the Arabic culture which is an historical culture" (144, citing Zaid). Even a "*lingua sacra* scripture", argues Wansbrough, "must be analyzed as a unit of literary production" (Wansbrough, 118); Graham and Kermani write, "if the miracle of the Qur'an is the language of revelation, then the language of the Qur'an has to be analyzed in literary terms and, to prove its superiority, be compared to other texts, especially poetry" (Graham and Kermani, 130). While commenting that unlike Western scholars, Muslims do not usually speak about a "history of the Qur'an", the text, in Esack's view, is "not free from a history and a context". This is why this book's basic premise is that a better understanding of that history and context may lead to our grasping "some approximation of its meaning" (2005, 192).

Tafsir: Qur'anic Exegesis

At 3: 7 the Qur'an speaks of some passages being clear and easy, while others have hidden meanings. My own take on this is that allegorical verses remind us that the totality of who God is lies beyond human comprehension; at the heart of God there is a profound mystery. Traditionally, Muslims distinguish *Muhkamat* (clear) from *Mutashabihat* (allegorical) verses. To render *Mutashabihat*, as some do, as "unclear" contradicts the many passages that describe the Qur'an as "clear". Only *Mukhamat* verses can inform legal decisions. Many Muslims also interpret verses on two levels, the literal (external) level (*zahir*) and the spiritual (internal) level (*batin*). *Tafsir* began during the lifetime of Muhammad, who encouraged his companions to study and interpret passages as well as to recite and memorize them. Muhammad was regarded as the best human interpreter of the Qur'an, one whose exegesis was inspired. He rejected the idea that everything he said was inspired (see Zakaria, 7) but he did claim inspiration on matters pertinent to his mission. This is why his acts and words, *ahadith* (accounts) were later recorded, giving us one of the sources for the situations of revelation. In English, the singular *hadith* is more commonly used. The best *tafsir*, though, is when the Qur'an sheds lights on its own meaning. The third best *tafsir* was by Muhammad's companions, not least of all Ibn 'Abbas. On the other hand, despite the fact that *tafsir* is almost as old as the text it seeks to illuminate, Muslims have always regarded *tafsir* as a somewhat risky enterprise; "to teach exegesis (*tafsir*) is inevitably to tread on dangerous theological grounds, to court the hubris and heresy of claiming to know God's intent". For this reason, it "is not a required course in traditional theological colleges" yet "every Muslim must engage in it" (Fischer and Abedi, 184). Traditional commentaries, often 10 or even 20 volumes, tend to follow a standard format. The commentator discusses each chapter sequentially, asking, "Was this *surah* revealed in Mecca or Madinah? What prompted its revelation? Can we explain the grammatical peculiarities in certain verses? Why is there repetition of certain words or phrases? ... Does the passage carry legal consequences ...?" (McAuliffe, 184). Depending on the particular interests of the commentator or on the specific passage under discussion, commentary may focus on "grammar, law, mystical reflection" or "theology" (McAuliffe, 183). Traditional commentators also discuss the opinions of earlier exegetes. Many older editions of the Qur'an were accompanied by the commentary of al-Bardawi (d. 1316) (Leemhuis, 152).

Another approach is to privilege "intra-quranic interpretation and that which can be grounded in the statements of the Prophet and his closest companions" (McAuliffe, 200), pursued by such modern commentators as Sayyid Qutb and Mawdudi. Qutb's *In the Shade of the Qur'an* is available online (see References) and is well worth browsing. Mawdudi's *Chapter Introductions* are also online. The influential ibn Kathir (d. 1373) was less interested in reproducing insights "accumulated during the centuries" of *tafsir* scholarship, which he bypassed. A student of the *salafist* Ibn Taymiyya, Ibn Kathir asks what did the earliest generations (the *salafuun*, the first generation, their children and their grandchildren) understand? Qutb and others distrust medieval commentators, whom they view as too tied to the interests of corrupt political leaders, just as some contemporary Muslims distrust traditionally trained scholars. Until recently, translations of *tafsir* into English have been rare. I decided to use, as a traditional source, Ibn Kathir, whose commentary is available in an abridgment of ten volumes. Concerned with avoiding innovation (*bida*), he aims to give the earliest opinion, so often cites Ibn 'Abbas, whose commentary, with others, is now available as part the Great Commentaries of the Holy Qur'an series, published by the Royal Al-Bayt Institute for Islamic Thought of Jordan. For modern *tafsir*, I draw on a range of writings, many of which are not commentaries in the traditional sense but deal with relevant passages as they discuss different aspects of Muslim thought. One modern, conservative commentary I consult is Muhammad al-Ghazali's *Thematic Commentary*. Al-Ghazali, recipient of many awards, taught at leading Muslim universities until his death in 1996. Saeed (2006) includes Ghazali as a Muslim who went "beyond the traditionally accepted *tafsir* methods" (13). Al-Ghazali does not discuss every *ayah* but concentrates on what he sees as the organic unity of each chapter. I also make wide use of Ali (2001). Ali, who consulted a range of famous commentaries, says that "in translating the Text", which was for him a lifetime labour of love, he "aired no views of" his "own, but followed the received commentaries". "Where they differed among themselves", he chose what appeared to "be the most reasonable opinion" (Ali, xii). Ali rarely sources his annotations, so it is impossible to track most of these to the "received commentaries". There are times, too, when he does give his own view.

Sources for Situations of Revelation

The main sources of information for the situations of revelations are the biographies of Muhammad. Here, what is generally considered to be the earliest and most reliable account was written by Ibn Ishaq (d. 767) although the version that survived was a later edition edited by Ibn Hisham (d. 833). Given the time gap between Muhammad's death and this *sira* (biography) some scholars are dubious about its reliability. Ibn Ishaq himself was apt to comment "it is alleged" or "only god knows the truth" if he was unsure of the historicity of an account (Guillaume, xiv). Ibn Ishaq does include accounts of miraculous happenings, which Western scholars assume have no factual basis. The version I use throughout what follows is Guillaume's 1955 translation, which attempted to restore the original "as it left" Ibn Ishaq's "pen or was dictated ... to his hearers" (xxx). I also consult a modern composite *sira* by Martin Lings which draws, in addition to Ibn Ishaq, on other early sources, such as al-Tabari (d. 923), whose *History* covered portions of Muhammad's life. These sources were not subject to the more rigorous scrutiny and testing for authenticity that was applied to the *hadith*, although *sira* is, broadly, a category of *hadith* literature. Unlike *hadith*, *sira* has no legal consequences. From at least soon after the *hijrah*, Muhammad's companions began to memorize and record his words; these interpreted the Qur'an and also sometimes extended the scope of Qur'anic verses. In the years after Muhammad's death, Muslims were well aware that people invented and doctored *hadith* for their own purposes. People known as traditionalists (*muhaditheen*) then began to compile semi-official collections. Complex rules for inclusion were developed. Most important was establishing a chain of narration traced back to a wife, relative or companion of Muhammad. Not only must the source be a pious, honest Muslim but each link in the chain had to meet the same qualification. Attestation by more than one source or the existence of several chains of narration (*isnad*) was also important. A break in the chain was serious, although the *hadith* might still be included. Less attention was paid to content (*matn*) due to the large number of *hadith*, although criteria concerning content were applied. Muhammad did not predict the future, or promise reward or punishment disproportionate to the act concerned, for example. Nor did he ever contradict the Qur'an. Among Sunni Muslims, six *hadith* collections became accepted as "sound" (*sahih*); Shi'a accept four collections. Even within these collections, *hadith* are further classified as *hasan* (noble, good) and *da'if* (weak). The latter can be used for exhortation but not as the basis for a legal decision. The most famous Sunni collection was by al-Bukhari (d. 870), who sifted through 600,000 *hadith* before selecting 7,275 (of which 2,762 are repeated at least once). Some *hadith* can be dated or linked with specific historical contexts, but many contain no clues about their original circumstances. Largely, this is because compilers were interested in the universal aspects of the Qur'an and of Muhammad's message, so they collected *hadith* under categories such as prayer, fasting, war, revelation with no attempt at reconstructing an historical sequence. The edition of Bukhari that I consulted is the revised edition of Khan's English–Arabic interlinear translation (1987), which is searchable online at www.usc.edu/dept/MSA/fundamentals/hadithsunnah/bukhari/. I reference the Book and *hadith* number. If a *hadith* is unreferenced (such as the two cited above) it is because, although very widely cited, they are frequently left unsourced, so tracking them is a major task. A search did not locate these in any of the six main collections. Despite the rigour with which the six collections were compiled, "unlike the issue of the Qur'an's authenticity, the debate" says Esack "on the *sunnah* as authoritative has generally been a free for all, even in Muslim circles" (2005, 120). Muir's historical reconstruction and dating of events is also useful, despite his negative attitude towards his subject. I consulted the 1912 abridged edition of his *Life of Mohammad*. I did a lot of work on Muir during my doctoral research, so I am grateful to my mentors, whose influence always informs my writing.

Outline of This Book

Any discussion of the Qur'an needs to explore how Muhammad first became aware of his prophetic mission, experienced revelation and received the Qur'an. Early *surahs*, following the order of revelation, tell us a lot about this, as well as about the basic monotheistic and ethical message proclaimed by Muhammad. The first chapter, which summarizes roughly half the verses revealed at Mecca, is entitled 'The Prophet's Call'. The early verses also tell us a lot about Islam's doctrines of God and of humanity, about the type of conduct God expects and about the nature of the Qur'an itself. The second chapter, paraphrasing verses revealed at Mecca up until approximately 619 or 620, is entitled "The Qur'an on God, Humanity and Itself". While the migration (622 CE) from Mecca to Medina was a crucial defining moment, the next chapter discusses the final segment of Meccan verses and the first sequence of Medinan verses. Entitled "The Community Takes Shape", this chapter deals with Surah 22, which permitted self-defence for the first time. My discussion suggests continuity between the end of the Meccan and the start of the Medinan periods. The *hijrah* is best understood by discussing what happened before and after rather than by isolating it at the start of a new chapter. It was at Medina that The Prophet's mosque was built, the name Islam revealed and the five daily prayers established. The direction of prayer was changed from Jerusalem to Mecca, thus the community started to differentiate itself from Judaism and from Christianity. Many passages relating to how the Other should be viewed belong to this segment, so a sub-theme is "Attitudes to the Religious Other". Chapter 4 turns to the remaining *surahs* under the heading "The Community Consolidates". Chapters 3 and 4 include most passages containing legal material, such as Surah 4 on women and 9 on war, as well as Surah 5, which has the penalty for theft. Far from the Qur'an being a book full of rules and regulations, there are actually only a handful of verses that can properly be classified as "legal". Saeed (2006) says that estimates of the number of legal verses ranges "from 80 to 500, depending on the definition of 'legal'" and if the higher estimate is preferred, most "refer to … forms of worship and ritual" (65). Chapter 4 also explores governance and what we might call "mosque–state relations" at this stage in the development of the community. All four chapters follow the biography of the Prophet and so reflect his developing self-understanding, beginning with his call to preach in private, then in public, then to become leader of a distinct community. Here, verses indicating his prophetic authority appear. A final chapter describes how the Qur'an is used within Muslim faith and practice, touching on the arts of *tajwid* (recitation) and *khatt* (calligraphy). It also summarizes in more detail Muslim conviction about the Qur'an as "eternal" and briefly visits some debates about interpretation raised in previous discussions.

1 The Prophet's Call

First Revelation

According to the traditional chronology, Muhammad was 40 years old when he experienced his call to preach God's word. The first segment of the Qur'an, 96: 1–5, is associated with this event. Muhammad, born in 570 CE in Mecca, in what is now Saudi Arabia, was orphaned in childhood. His father, Abdullah, died before he was born. His mother, Aminah, died when he was six. Although a member of the powerful Quraysh clan, Muhammad certainly experienced insecurity and hardship as an orphan, inheriting very little from his parents. For the first two years of his life he was suckled by a nurse, Halima, mainly in the desert. According to custom, Bedouin boys from the city were raised in this manner to accustom them to the rhythm and ways of the desert. Infections common in urban centres were also more easily avoided. At first, Aminah had difficulty finding anyone willing to foster an orphan. No fee was due for performing this service but foster mothers expected some favour in return. Halimah agreed to foster Muhammad because she sensed that greatness lay in his future. She cared for him as if he were one of her own children. Until Muhammad was eight, his grandfather, Abdul Muttalib, was his guardian. The Quraysh were hereditary guardians of what was then a pagan shrine, the Ka'bah, which was a major source of income. Ancient Arab traditions associate this with Abraham and Ishmael; Muslims believe it was the original monotheist sanctuary. By now, it houses numerous idols. Muhammad's grandfather, a senior and respected member of the clan, was responsible for taking care of pilgrims. He rediscovered the sacred well of Zamzan from which Hagar and Ishmael had quenched their thirst. Muhammad's family traced its lineage back to Abraham. When Abdul Muttalib died, his brother, Abu Talib, assumed responsibility for Muhammad. Abu Talib was not as affluent as his father, so Muhammad was expected to earn his upkeep. He did so mainly as a shepherd. The tradition comments that "there is no prophet but who has tended a flock", which serves to establish Muhammad's *bone fides* as a prophet "like unto Moses" (Guillaume, 72). Later, Muhammad accompanied his uncle on a trading mission to Syria. In his mid-20s, he was employed by Khadijah, a wealthy widow and business-woman, to supervise another mission to Syria. After successfully leading this venture, Khadijah asked Muhammad to become her husband. She was 40. He was 25. They were married.

By this time, Muhammad had acquired a reputation for honesty, earning the nickname *al-amin* (the trustworthy). Tradition relates a story about the Ka'bah being rebuilt after a flood. When clan leaders began to argue over who would have the honour of lifting the black-stone back into its place, they agreed to adjudication. This task fell to Muhammad, who was 35 at the time. Muhammad's quick-thinking diplomacy prevented the clans from conflict. Placing his cloak on the ground, then the stone on the cloak, he asked each clan leader to take hold of the cloak to help raise the stone towards its place in the corner of the shrine. Then, as mutually agreed, Muhammad himself slipped the stone into its niche (Guillaume, 86).

Although surrounded by idolatry, Muhammad was unhappy with the polytheistic religion of his peers. He may have identified with the *hanifs*, who quietly maintained monotheism despite the difficulty of doing so in a society dominated by pagan practices and beliefs. Abdul Muttalib had presided at pagan rites but may have done so more to honour the pilgrims than to venerate idols and pagan deities. Lings writes, "God" was "the great reality" for him. He was "no doubt nearer to the religion of Abraham than most of his contempo-raries" (Lings, 16). Muhammad was also unhappy with the treatment of the most vulnerable people in society, whose welfare was neglected by the elite. There was a wide gap between rich and poor. Justice was a rare commodity, since wealth paid for judicial decisions. As Muhammad approached his 40th birthday, he spent more and more time in retreat, praying and meditating in a cave on Mount Hira, some distance from Mecca. In the year 610, during the last ten days of the month of Ramadan, on what became known as the "Night of Power", Muhammad experienced his call to become God's final prophet.

He is said to have entered a deep meditative state, during which he became conscious of a man, or of the form of a man, standing in front of him, holding a piece of cloth or silk. The man said, "*Iqra*", "read" or "recite". Muhammad replied that he could not; according to Muslim tradition, Muhammad was illiterate. This will be discussed later in this book. Again, the man told Muhammad to read. He repeated that he could not. When the command

"*Iqra*" was repeated for the third time, Muhammad was compelled to recite the words, which were now somehow burnt into his heart. "Recite" he said, "in the name of the Lord who created humanity from a clot of blood, who teaches humanity by the Pen what he does not know." These opening words place both God and creation at the centre of the Qur'an's message. The first word to be recited, "*Iqra*" gives us the name of the scripture. Ali says that the command to "recite" implies "not only the duty of blazoning forth Allah's message" but "also the duty of promulgation and wide dissemination" (1672). God, through Gabriel, reveals God's word to the prophet, who recites or proclaims this. God is "cherisher and creator". Creation itself is the source of knowledge about God; it is God's first revelation. The Arabs had a concept of Allah as the supreme deity, but this Allah was remote, uninterested in human life. Although Allah is masculine in terms of syntax this does not mean that Muslims conceive of God as a male; God cannot be compared with any other being. As we learn more and more about the Allah of the Qur'an, Allah is revealed to be intimately concerned with human life. Allah is the only God, not one among others, which is implied by the term "supreme". Allah is not mean or neglectful but "bountiful", a God who meets human needs. God has been described as the "subject" of the Qur'an in a double sense. First, God is the author of the Qur'an. Use of "I" and "we" in the Qur'an warns against any attempt to reduce God to a simplistic formulation, or from "being defined in anthropomorphic terms" (Sells, 20). Second, God can be explained as the main subject-matter of the Qur'an; God is situated at the centre of "attention" of the Qur'an (see Madigan, 79). The Surah is named *al-'Alaq* "the clot" (from verse 2) or "*Iqra*" from the opening word. Qur'an is also derived from the word for "city". Therefore, a whole civilization can be said to rest on the Book. Islam embraces the political and the spiritual.

Reference to "the pen" (*qalam*) and to "teaching" reveal that God is also a God who instructs; God ensures that women and men know God's will, so that they can live lives that please God. God's will is always understood in Islam as distinguishing right from wrong, what is *permitted* from the what is *prohibited*. Those who please God live moral lives; those who please God do what is right and refrain from what is wrong. The notion of the "pen" is substantial, permanent; God's word is not a mere fleeting communication but an enduring message. Already, although it is a "recitation" and would not be "written down" at this early stage, the Qur'an is aware of its future status as a Book, or scroll. The pen, says Ali, symbolizes a "permanent revelation", one that is also to become a written record. Lings links the pen with the "celestial archetype" of the Qur'an that had been penned by angels in heaven (45). Muhammad tells us that he was shaken and confused by the experience. He had an intense dislike of the *kahini*, the Soothsayers. In his view, these shamans faked their spiritual encounters, or were possessed by evil not good spirits. He feared that his experience had an evil cause. As he stumbled, trembling as if from severe cold, down the mountain, he briefly thought of throwing himself off so that he could "gain rest", but resisted this (Guillaume, 106). Non-Muslim critics regard this as a sign of Muhammad's mental instability, which they also link with his experiences of revelation. Often described as "trances", they attribute these to epilepsy or to some type of malady. Others explain his "trances" as self-induced shaman-like ecstasy. Muslims, for their part, do not see any cause to criticize or to censure Muhammad for what may have been a fleeting thought of unworthiness to serve God, rather as Jeremiah cursed the day of his birth, and wished himself dead (Jeremiah 20: 14).

The experience in the cave was profound and perplexing. As he ran down the mountain, the Angel reappeared, saying, "Muhammad, you are God's messenger, and I am Gabriel" (Guillaume, 106). Wherever Muhammad looked, he saw Gabriel's presence. When he finally returned home, Khadijah wrapped him in his cloak. Some sources say that Khadijah sent servants to look for him because of his long absence. Later, Muhammad's cloak became a symbol of his prophetic office, and of the authority of successive leaders of the Muslim community. Still trembling, Muhammad related what he had experienced to Khadijah. Her immediate response was to assure Muhammad that he was neither insane nor demon-possessed, but that God had called him to become the prophet of his people. Quickly, she consulted her cousin, Warraqah, a Christian, who confirmed her opinion that Muhammad was the promised prophet "like unto Moses" (Deuteronomy 18: 18) (Guillaume, 107). Renowned for his knowledge of scripture, Warraqah had long expected that God would call an Arab prophet. He believed that the angel whom Muhammad had encountered was the same divine messenger who had spoken to Moses. In the New Testament, Gabriel announces the births of John the Baptist and of Jesus. From the *hadith*, we learn how Muhammad would drip with sweat, even on bitterly cold nights, when Gabriel appeared. Sometimes, he would hear a bell ring, warning him that a revelation was coming (Bukhari, 1: 2). He later said that he could only distinguish where one revelation ended and another began when Gabriel recited the *bismillahi*. Often, he heard and saw Gabriel, but at other times the words were "burnt" onto his heart, as they were for Jeremiah (Jeremiah 20: 9). Revelation would often come when he was wrapped in his cloak.

Muhammad then consulted Warraqah himself, who confirmed his conviction that Muhammad was now God's prophet. People, he predicted, would revile him, reject him, slander him, call him a liar, but as long as he lived Warraqah would help his cause. This tradition about Warraqah builds on earlier episodes in Muhammad's life when various monks recognized him as the promised or expected Arab prophet. In this view, God had raised prophets up among other nations while the Arabs still waited for their prophet. Stories associated with Muhammad's birth depict a light shining from Aminah, who experienced no birth pains, illuminating the far-off castle of Basra. A voice announced, "you are pregnant with the lord of this people" (Guillaume, 69). A Jew saw a star under which "Ahmad" would be born (70). When Muhammad was two and still fostered by Halimah, two men dressed in white came to him while he was asleep, opened his breast, removed his heart, cleaned it, replaced it and washed his chest. This is said to have left a small mark between his shoulder-blades. Muhammad's heart was thus prepared to receive divine revelation (71–2). When he accompanied his uncle on the trading mission to Syria, he encountered a Nestorian monk, Bahira, who, recognizing the mark of prophecy on his shoulders, predicted that the boy would become his people's prophet and must be protected (80). Also on a trade mission to Syria, the first in Khadijah's employment, he fell asleep while resting under a tree. Another monk saw him asleep and enquired who it was who was resting there because "none but a prophet ever sat under that tree" (82). Tradition regards Surah 96 as Muhammad's call as a prophet but not yet to public ministry. At this point, he confided in family and friends. Khadijah is universally acknowledged as the first believer. The first male believer was probably Ali, Muhammad's cousin and son-in-law, whose cause Shi'a Islam later championed as the legitimate successor to the leadership of Islam. Ibn Ishaq identified Abu Bakr, Muhammad's future father-in-law and the first Sunni caliph, as the second adult male convert although some sources list him as the first (Guillaume, 114). This reflects later Shi'a–Sunni rivalry. Abu Bakr was a powerful and prominent member of the Quraysh, in contrast to many early followers (known as companions, *sahaba*) who were poor and socially insignificant. Another early follower was Muhammad's former slave, Zaid. Surah 26: 214 "warn your family" may date from this period (Lings, 50) although the rest of 26 is 111 in Zarkarsh's sequence.

The Second Revelation

Following Zarkarsh, the second passage is 68, which came to Muhammad with words of comfort and reassurance; he was neither insane nor demon-possessed. The *surah* begins with the letter *NUN*. This is one of the so-called "cryptic" or "abbreviated letters" with which 29 chapters begin. These are mainly later Meccan chapters. These letters might have been used to attract Muhammad's attention, like the ringing of the bell. Some describe them as alternative names for Muhammad. Others suggest that they function to invoke mystery, awareness that the Qur'an enters the world from the "unseen" (*al-ghayb*), that the totality of God will always remain unknowable. God, says 3: 179, does not reveal the secrets of the unseen. Categorized as "allegorical", others say that only God knows the meaning of these letters. They are included in the Qur'an because they were revealed to Muhammad, so properly form part of its content. Surah 68 takes it name from the "Pen" which again invokes the concepts of propagation and of permanency. Later, the Qur'an affirms that while mistakes and errors may have corrupted the content of earlier scriptures revealed to previous prophets, the Qur'an is error-free. Even though all scriptures contain the same essential message, this message is expressed comprehensively, reliably and definitively in the Qur'an. "By the pen" represents the first "divine oath". God swears by the "written record" that Muhammad is neither insane nor possessed. Divine oaths feature in the Qur'an as a summons for men and women to apply reason, to recognize God as the author of life. These divine oaths often invoke the natural world. In the Qur'an, the natural world functions as a "sign" of God's grace and blessing. People, however, are never to swear by nature, only by God's Name. God can invoke nature because God created nature; for people to invoke nature implies that nature is itself divine. The opening cryptic letter, *NUN* resembles an ink-pot, which, says Nasr, reminds us of the ink used, figuratively, to pen the heavenly Book (Nasr, 25). Others have it that the Pen was God's first creation, followed by the Book so that God could publish "what he had destined concerning good and evil" (Rippin and Knappert, 60–1).

Reference to the pen and to a "written record" illustrates the self-consciousness of the Qur'an as a permanent message. The implication, too, is that it is coherent and rational, not the babbling of a *kahini*. Muhammad is highly honoured and exalted; very soon people will see that it is those who reject his message who are mad, not Muhammad, who must resist their attempts to bend him to their will. Muhammad's opponents speak falsehood so that they can continue their selfish, cruel, godless lives. Slandering Muhammad, their pride prevents them from realizing their own human limitations. Next, we hear the first story, or narrative, related in the Qur'an. This describes what happens when people forget God, relying instead on their own abilities. People plant a beautiful orchard. One day, as the fruit matures, they go to sleep planning to harvest their fruit in the morning, but omit to say "by God's leave" (*insha allah*). That night, God sends a storm; in the morning, the orchard is "dark and desolate" with no fruit left to pick. Realizing their error, the people repent. God promises that he will now bless them with an even better garden. Next, the chapter extends the promise of "Gardens" to all those who live righteous lives. Allah is a just God, so sinners and the righteous will be treated differently. Pagans appear to think that they enjoy a covenant with God, that regardless of the lives they live, God will reward them (see Chapter 4 for "covenant" in the Qur'an). In this, they are misguided. Certainly, no "Book" (*Kitab*) offers them any such assurance. Both the idea that pagans enjoy a covenant with God and that they possess a scripture promising them salvation irrespective of moral conduct is ludicrous. No scripture can promise that the faithful and the faithless will receive the same reward. As for the wicked, no witness will argue their cause on the Day of Judgement. Nor can anyone hope for assistance from any "partner" in the Godhead, because none exist. This very early passage is probably a rejection of the Christian notion of the Trinity, although pagans also believed in divine partners. This *surah* begins with Muhammad as its audience before shifting first to pagans and then to Christians. Muhammad may have expected Christian support because of his experiences with Bahira and Warraqah. Warraqah, incidentally, remained a Christian, but Muslims always speak of him with respect.

On the one hand, those who worship false gods can only expect retribution. On the other, it is such people who often seem to prosper. This, says Surah 68, is because prosperity now is a false sign. God allows people to damn themselves by further transgression, or to take the opportunity to repent. As the Qur'an's theme of judgement develops, this is always set alongside the promise of forgiveness and mercy to the repentant. Above all, God is merciful. A biblical reference follows next, the first so far; Jonah, having defied God's command to preach to the people of Nineveh, ended up in the belly of a large fish. Then he repented and was forgiven. Repentance and forgiveness also followed when he finally preached in Nineveh. Jonah is considered a prophet in Islam, the first of 25 named in the Book. Like Muhammad, he is both a prophet (*nabi*) and a messenger (*rasul*). The latter receive a *kitab* (a book).

Rasul are sent to their own people with a fresh revelation. The final verses turn again to Muhammad, encouraging him to be patient, unlike Jonah. His enemies dismiss him as possessed, yet in reality he has been entrusted with a "message for the whole world". Earlier messengers, including Jonah, had messages for particular people at particular times, but Muhammad is the universal prophet; his message will remain valid until the end of time. Muhammad, the prophet of his people, was an Arab prophet who received a message in Arabic. However, the Qur'an is explicit from this early point about the universal scope of his mission.

The Silence

After Surah 68, a period of silence followed. Sources describe this as between six months and two years in length. As unnerving as this silence was, Muhammad remained patient. When the next revelation came, it was one of assurance. Called the "Cloaked", Surah 73 addressed Muhammad as the one "wrapped up" in his cloak. Muhammad is to pray during the night, reciting or chanting the Qur'an in "measured tones". At this stage, only 96: 1–5; 68; 26: 214; and possibly 74 (which may have preceded 73) existed. However, Muhammad may already have tried to rush recitation, or to speak too rapidly as he received segments from Gabriel. The words of the Qur'an are so profound and powerful that not only would it destroy Muhammad to receive all 114 chapters at once, but the content is to be savoured, pronounced slowly. The notion of the power of God's word is also biblical; Jeremiah 23: 29 says, "Is not my Word like a fire ... that breaks the rock into pieces." Night is best for prayer, "potent for governing the soul". Verse 9 describes Allah as the only God, "There is no God but God." This is close to the declaration of faith, Islam's first pillar that proclaims, "There is no God but God." God is, says verse 9, Lord of East and West. Leave God to deal with those who deny God, even if they appear to prosper, because he is ready to deal with them when the time is right. Their fetters are already waiting for them. Picking up on the ending of Surah 68, this chapter turns to address the whole human race, to which Muhammad has been sent. We now encounter the first of many references to Pharaoh, usually the Pharaoh whom Moses challenged, although Moses is not specifically named here. Pharaoh rejected the messenger and was punished. Parallels are drawn between Moses and Muhammad; both were shepherds, both received Books, both had to deal with opposition and back-sliding. Both led their people on a journey. Those who reject Muhammad's message will face punishment, as surely as the day will come when the sky itself splits apart. This is a favourite Qur'anic phrase. People who choose to follow Muhammad's straight path (a synonym for Islam, or for right conduct), however, will reach Allah. Verse 20 might be of Medinan origin; it enjoins regular prayer and charity, and recommends night prayer, reading as much of the Qur'an as an individual can manage and "striving in Allah's cause" (*yuqatiloona fee sabeeli Allahi*). This, says Ali, refers to *jihad*, the inner, spiritual struggle and external good acts although here the word *qital* not *jihad* is used. Allah understands when illness or travel interrupts prayer.

Surahs 73 and 74 are taken (with the end of 68) as Muhammad's commission to begin public preaching. Again, he is addressed as "wrapped in his cloak". He is to "rise up and warn". He is now to preach to the many, not to the few. The time for self-pity, for introspection, is over. He is to be courageous, bold and fearless. "Turn to God", he is to thunder, and "avoid the distress of Judgement Day". Power, wealth and status are all God's gifts yet sinners persistently want more and more, through greed. They thrive on others' praise, even though they turn away from God. They ridicule God's message as the "words of a mortal" and God's messenger as a trickster. This almost certainly reflects Muhammad's experience as he began his public preaching, and was denounced and ridiculed; Ibn Ishaq records that people "called him a liar, insulted him, and accused him of being a sorcerer, a diviner, of being possessed" (Guillaume, 130). Possibly, 96: 6–19 can be inserted here. These verses focus on people's arrogance; they think they are self-sufficient, with no need for God. Not only do such people rebel against God's laws but they try to prevent others from obeying God as well. Such people even think they can rely on their social prestige to ward off God's wrath. This, though, will be of no use whatsoever. Here, 96 refers specifically to Abu Jahl, a Quraysh who had become one of Muhammad's most implacable enemies. Verse 17 suggests that when God sends angels to punish the man who prevented Muhammad from praying at the Ka'bah as a sinner and as a liar, dragging him by his forelock, he will try to summon the "council" to aid him. This is the Quraysh junta, or clan-council that at the time governed the city in the absence of a supreme chief. Abu Jahl may already have physically attacked some of Muhammad's companions, even though Muhammad himself, under his uncles' protection, was never personally attacked. There is a story of Abu Jahl attempting to attack him, only to find that his hand withered around the stone he intended to hit Muhammad with. It dropped harmlessly to the ground (Guillaume, 135).

Abu Jahl began the practice, which later became official policy, of boycotting the businesses of Muhammad's followers (Guillaume, 145). The Quraysh also tried to bribe Muhammad to abandon his preaching, offering him money or leadership of the clan (Guillaume, 133). Surah 74: 5 tells Muhammad to avoid all abominations. This is understood to refer to observing Jewish dietary rules and other rules about ritual cleanliness, such as washing before prayer. We know from 73: 6 that Muhammad prayed regularly; it is assumed that his followers imitated his example. Lings suggests that at this point the five-daily prayers were established, although this is normally dated after the migration (Lings, 47). Prayer at this time may have consisted of kneeling, prostrating and touching the forehead to the grounds (Sells, 18). Revelations now begin to come in rapid succession. Surah 74 contains the most detailed description so far of the fires of hell, guarded by 19 angels. Angels, who are servants of God in the Qur'an, perform various functions such as guarding hell, greeting the resurrected dead on Judgement Day and recording our deeds. Section two contains a set of divine oaths – by the sun, by the moon, by the dawn – as God points to signs of God's ownership of all that is, warning that every soul will be asked to account for its deeds. Those who failed to pray, to feed the hungry, to acknowledge the Day of Judgement, will have no intercessor for them. Here, the link between turning towards God in worship, and helping the needy, begins to emerge. Verse 52 says that the unbelievers claim they would believe if they too were to receive a "scroll". There is evidence that the Quraysh leaders said they would support Muhammad if Muhammad's God would speak to them as well. They could not accept that God was speaking to a relatively insignificant member of their clan, instead of its leaders.

Persecution and Asylum

Surah 111, possibly fourth, "The Twisted Rope" or noose is set firmly in the context of persecution. It begins, "perish the hands of the Father of Flame". This is one of only a few specific references to Muhammad's enemies. The Father of Flame was Abu Lahab, an uncle of Muhammad who was renowned for his foul temper, hence his nickname. Lahab pressurized Abu Talib to abandon his protection of Muhammad, which he resisted. Lahab's wife "carries twisted firewood" but was actually preparing for the eternal fire, figuratively placing a noose around her own neck. Skilfully scorning the Fires, the *surah* puns their nickname. When Mrs Fire heard these words, she threatened to smash her stone pestle across Muhammad's face. As he had lampooned her, she would write a poem in his honour as well, "We disobey the reprobate, Flout the commands he doth recite, and his religion hate" (Guillaume, 161). Surah 81, "The Folding Up", an eloquent, rhythmic *surah*, is an example of the use of metaphor. The first eight verses start with "When": "When the sun is folded up, when the falling stars loose their lustre, when the mountains vanish, when the she-camels with ten-month-old calves are left untended ..." Verses 8 to 9 ask how the infant girl killed at birth will answer when asked what crime she had committed? The Qur'an condemns infanticide, which was common in pre-Islamic Arabia. When the earth is rolled back like a scroll to reveal both the heavens and the Fire of Hell, every soul will learn its fate. What appears fixed and solid will be "folded up" as easily as a scroll. A similar metaphor is used at 21: 104 which says that the universe was unfolded like a scroll, so one day will be rolled back again. God, who created the world, will also wind it up. Surah 73: 14 referred to how, on that Day, the mountains will become sand, "poured out and flowing down". The melting away of mountains is also a biblical motif (see Micah 1: 5). Even the planets in the night sky will recede. Muhammad, as God's messenger, affirms that all this is true. Those who listen will inherit eternal life. Muhammad "your companion" is not possessed but an honourable messenger, which suggests that this segment was addressing the believers. Gabriel, who brings him revelation, holds high rank in the heavens, where he has authority. Muhammad's message is intended for the whole earth, again stressing Muhammad's universal mission. Similarity between the style of the Qur'an and the utterances of the *Kahini* did not pass unnoticed. Ibn Ishaq frequently refers to claims that Muhammad was bewitched, or that he fabricated his messages (Guillaume, 130). In fact, says the Qur'an, Muhammad's message comes from God, from the very Throne of the Lord (see Conclusion for discussion of "Throne"). Others defended Muhammad, "'He is a poet.' 'No, he is no poet, for we know poetry ...' 'He is a sorcerer', 'No, we have heard sorcerers and their sorcery, and there is no splitting of knots'" (Guillaume, 121).

Surah 87, "The Most High", provides insight into the "character" or "nature" of the Most High God. God not only created the universe but also watches over it, orders its laws and understands creatures' needs, unlike the Allah of pre-Islamic Arabia. Many Arabs thought that arbitrary, impersonal *Zaman* (time) determined human fate. Muhammad is a "reminder". People have plenty of signs of God's reality in nature as well as in the messages of earlier prophets. Regarding itself as the religion of nature (*din al-fitrah*) Islam teaches that being Muslim, or obedient to God, is natural. To become Muslim is to revert rather than to convert, to return to what our natures know is the truth. Our tendency to forget causes us to stray yet we naturally know the difference between right and wrong. Muhammad points us towards the correct path; the choice to follow or to reject Muhammad is personal; the prophet can compel nobody, nor wished to. The path is easy but we must each take the first step along the way. Those who purify themselves and remember (*dhikr*) God will follow Muhammad. Remembering is a major Qur'anic motif; remember what befell those who scorned God's word; remember God's mercy; remember God's generosity through nature. Those who prefer this world will ignore Muhammad. Verses 18–19 identify Muhammad as the successor of Abraham and Moses. Although Moses was alluded to in Surah 73, this is the first time we encounter his name. Among the 25 prophets named in the Qur'an, Abraham and Moses are especially significant in establishing Muhammad's prophetic *bone fides*. The complete story of Moses' life is not recounted; parts of his narrative are told at: 2: 49–61; 7: 103–60; 10: 75–93; 17: 101–4; 20: 9–97; 26: 10–66; 27: 7–14; 28: 3–46; 40: 23–30; 43: 46–55; 44: 17–31; and 79: 15–25. Moses is mentioned more than any other prophet (136 times), followed by Abraham (referred to in 25 chapters).

Surah 92, "The Night", warns about the fate of people who deny God, fleshing ethical conduct out in more detail. Since wealth and success are God's gifts, we must not be miserly but should give to the needy. Our wealth, if we are niggardly and greedy, will not prevent us from falling into the Pit. As a trust from God, wealth is not an absolute possession. At times, wicked people actually appear to flourish. As Muhammad's companions were persecuted by the rich and powerful, this observation would have been confirmed by experience. Here a light–dark, night–day metaphor is used, which repeats itself throughout the Qur'an. Just as night appears to obscure the day yet does not annihilate it, so at times evil appears to block out the good yet does not destroy it. As with Surah 68, God is assuring us that the victory of evil is only temporary. When the time is right, good will defeat evil. Verse 3 refers to the simultaneous creation of "male and female", a theme to which we return later. Here, this is offered as a sign of God's goodness to humanity, since even sex is God's free gift. "By the plurality of male and female" (Sells, 21) is one of the divine oaths. "By the Night" is the opening divine oath.

Beginning with "By the Dawn", which gives 89 its name, this *surah* adds ethical substance to Muhammad's message. People who in the past spurned God's prophets were punished. Among the great civilizations of the world that rejected prophets were the 'Ad (possibly Petra), which, as did Pharaoh's Egypt (our second reference to Pharaoh), ignored God's prophet. Now, these civilizations lie in ruin. People are mistaken in their self-sufficiency. Instead, feed the hungry, take care of orphans (this social duty was very close to the Messenger's heart), refrain from stealing from others' inheritance and from storing up treasure on earth. Parallels can be made with the many biblical verses demanding care of widows, orphans and the poor (see Jeremiah 7: 6; Isaiah 10: 1–3). What you love on earth will be ground into powder. On Judgement Day, it will be too late to say that you *would have done good deeds*. The time to act is now. Those who give of their plenty to others will hear God's invitation, "enter my house". The details of *zakat* (literally purification, payment to charity) come later, but already the duty of generosity and of social responsibility is explicit (Sells, 17). As Jeremiah preached, so did Muhammad, "if you oppress not the stranger, the fatherless, the widow and shed not innocent blood" you will dwell peacefully in the land (Jeremiah 7: 6–7). Obviously, the rich among the Quraysh found the idea that the poor had a claim on their wealth obnoxious. Muhammad's condemnation of idolatry was also a threat, given that much income came from pilgrims. Surah 89 also employs the night–day metaphor. Sometimes, the night evokes feelings of gloom, but when the dawn breaks, this is swept away. When we embrace God, God's light sweeps aside the darkness within us. That same light, though, can also destroy us if we fail to embrace God.

The message of Surah 93 initially speaks to Muhammad, perhaps when he was experiencing a dark night of the soul. Beginning with "By the Glorious Morning Light", which gives the *surah* its name, it asks, "Did I not find you an orphan and comfort you? Have I not guided you? Have I not made you secure and independent?" Therefore, treat orphans fairly and deal justly with those who seek help, unlike the Quraysh, who often failed to listen to any petitioner, assuming that all such people were lazy malingerers. If God has blessed you, spread this blessing to others. Be bountiful, like God. Surah 94 is only eight verses long. Called "The Expansion of the Breast", it declares that God has "cleansed" the Prophet's breast, probably referring to the incident described above (p. 28). Muhammad's heart is a pure receptacle for the word of God, which is "enshrined" there. Muslims believe that all prophets are sinless; only perfect men can transmit God's holy word. Gabriel would cleanse Muhammad's heart again before the event known as the Ascent. Surah 103 is very short, at only three verses. This chapter, which uses assonance very effectively, was among the first I learned by heart in Arabic. It begins with an oath, "By time". By time, humanity is in a state of loss (*Inna alinsana lafee khusrin*) except for those who persevere patiently in good works and uphold the truth (*watawasaw bialhaqqi, watawarsaw bialsabri*). Surah 100, "The Runners", has 11 verses. The language is rhythmic. Metaphor is again put to effective use. The eagerness of war-steeds to carry their masters into battle is negatively compared with people's reluctance to express gratitude to God for his gifts. When what is truly in their hearts is revealed, the wealth of the ungrateful, which they love instead of God, will be scattered as the enemy scatter before charging horses, panting as they run. Surah 108 is also another three-verse *surah*. Muhammad is assured that his future is guaranteed, so he is to pray and "sacrifice". *Nahr* means a flesh-offering, but this is understood to refer to the Prophet's deep, inner giving of himself to God, so that *taqwa* (God-consciousness) permeated every moment of his life. God-centred in thought, word and deed, he began everything he did with the *bismillahi*. Those who hate Muhammad will be cut off from any hope of eternal bliss. Bukhari cites Muhammad's saying that no one has faith unless "they love me more than his father, his children and all mankind" (Bukhari, 2: 14). Love of Muhammad is only a little below love of God. The title "abundance" refers to the overflowing fountain promised in paradise. Surah 102, "The Piling Up") has eight verses. A visit to the cemetery will quickly sober us up. If we think we can delay dealing with our spiritual health while we waste time on trivial matters, piling up wealth, we are mistaken. On Judgement Day, how we answer the question "What did you do for pleasure?" will reveal whether we wasted life, or spent our time wisely in fruitful pursuits.

Surah 107, "Helping Neighbours", says that feeding the hungry and caring for orphans are virtuous acts, especially if this involves self-sacrifice. Giving to charity to be recognized or praised by others is as hypocritical as praying ostentatiously without ever thinking about the object of our prayer. Islam emphasizes that without the right intent, no act of devotion has any value. We might pray all night and fast all day but gain nothing except wakefulness and hunger if our hearts are not centred on God. People who make a show of generosity are often actually miserly, failing to help people in other, less public ways. The last verse gives the *surah* its name; we are to respond generously to our neighbour's needs. Surah 109, "Those who Reject Faith", emphasizes that the choice between belief and unbelief is personal. Ultimately, there is a parting of the ways between those who worship and those who reject God. The words "I will not worship what you worship, nor will you worship what I worship" may have rejected a compromise proposal from the Quraysh, who suggested "that they should all practice both religions" (Lings, 91). The title of Surah 105, "The Elephant", refers to an event from 570 CE, Muhammad's birth-year. Abrahah Ashram, an Ethiopian governor who ruled the Yemen, invaded Arabia. His elephant-mounted army was so large that the Quraysh offered no resistance. Then a flock of birds passing overhead dropped stones, destroying the army and saving Mecca. Even as powerful a man as Abrahah could not withstand God's will. Surah 113 returns to the day–night motif, in which "night" represents "evil" and "day" the "good" and in a prayer-like style, invites believers to ward off superstition and sorcery by seeking refuge in Allah. The title, "Daybreak", is from verse 1. It may have been about this time that Muhammad sent some 80 followers, in several batches for their own safety, to seek asylum, or refuge, in Christian Ethiopia. We cannot be precise, but this event took place during 614. A second contingent was sent in 615. After these events, a significant conversion, that of Umar, took place, probably towards the beginning of 617. Between 617 and 619, an official ban or boycott was imposed against the believers. There is a problem here with the order I have chosen to follow, indeed with all four listed in Appendix 1. All place chapters 19 and 20 later – the two Muslims place them roughly in the low 40s while the two non-Muslims place them in the mid- to high 50s, in sequence of revelation. However, all place 53 earlier; the Muslims at 21 and 22; the non-Muslims at 28 and at 46, which is closer to 19 and 20. However, we know from the biographical record that 53 was revealed after the migration to Ethiopia (as the event was called) but before Umar's conversion. We also know that the refugees took with them a copy of, or knew by heart, Surah 19 and that Umar read a manuscript of 20. Stylistically, 19 and 20 are more similar to 53 than to the chapters so far summarized. All are longer, with more narrative and more biblical allusions. They do seem to belong closer to each other. Surah 18, also out of sequence in terms of the chronological schemes, may fit better here in terms of context–content analysis.

These three, lengthier *surahs* introduce themes that are expanded in the later Meccan passages. Next, according to Zarkashi, was 114, which Ibn Abbas placed at the end, followed by 112. The issue is, "Do I shift 53 closer to 19 and 20, or move 18 and 20 closer to 53?" The sequence from 45 onwards (56 following Zarkashi) fits events that happened around about 619 and 620, so these chapters appear to be well placed. What I have decided to do is to summarize the remaining chapters from part one, then to discuss 19, 18, 53, and 20 in that order at the beginning of Chapter 2.

Surah 114, "Mankind", follows 113 in invoking men (and *jinn*; described later) to seek refuge in God, who cherishes humanity. The whispering of Satan can thus be warded off.

The four verses of "Purity of Faith" (Surah 112) proclaim God's Oneness and condemn comparison of God with anything, implying that God can not be pictured or visually represented. Explicit rejection of the notion that God was fathered or is the father of children probably had Christians in mind. The language is similar to the Nicene Creed's description of the Son as "begotten, not made".

"He Frowned" (Surah 80) refers to an incident when Muhammad was interrupted by a blind man as he preached to the pagans. In a moment of impatience, he "frowned" and ignored him. In 42 verses, Muhammad is mildly rebuked for this, since the man had earnestly sought him out while the pagan leaders were hard-hearted in opposing him. Muhammad later held the blind man in high esteem. He would sometimes lead the prayers when Muhammad was absent from Medina (Lings, 139). Ibn Ishaq wrote, "I did not specify one person to the exclusion of another, so withhold not the message from him who seeks it, and do not waste time over one who does not want it" (Guillaume, 167). Verses 15–16 refer to scribes who are noble and pious, presumably a description of those who were now writing the revelations down as instructed by Muhammad.

The title of Surah 97, "The Night of Power", refers to the night when Surah 96 was revealed. The Night of Power is better than a thousand months. Angels descend on this night, sent down by God. It is a night of *salam*, peace. "Islam" is derived from the same root as "peace". It aims to establish peace on earth.

Surah 91, "The Sun", begins with a series of divine oaths; by the sun, by the day, by the night. People are summoned to heed God's word, unlike the Thamud (successors of the Ad), who rejected their prophet. We know from 7: 73 that the people of Thamud were cruel to animals, turning a female camel (referred to here in verse 13) away from her pasture. Pasture was regarded as common property, so the people had no right to deny one of God's creatures her food. These wicked people then crippled the camel. In retribution, God destroyed their city. Here, as in the book of Jonah, God reveals God's concern for animals as well as for people. In Jonah, when the people repented God did not destroy Nineveh, so many cattle were also saved. The she-camel parable is references at 7: 73, 77; 11: 64; 17: 59; 26: 155–7; 54: 27–29 and 91: 13.

Surah 85, "The Stars", takes its name from the opening divine oath to the signs of the zodiac. Invariably, people reject and oppose God's prophets merely because they believe in Allah. The unrepentant are hell-bound, but the repentant will experience God's forgiveness and mercy. God, who gave life, can also restore it at God's will. Pharaoh and the Thamud are again rebuked. Yet, despite awareness of what befell these people, many still refuse to repent. Verse 21 describes the Qur'an as glorious (*majeed*), inscribed on a preserved tablet (*fi lawhi mahfoodth*). This is the heavenly book, penned by angels from which Gabriel brings the revelations down to Muhammad. It also affirms the permanent and written nature of the Qur'an.

"The Fig" (Surah 95) has more divine oaths – "by the fig and the olive", "by Mount Sinai", "by the city of security", which refers to Mecca. Covenants between the Quraysh and Arab tribes guaranteed the security and safety of the city, where no arms or weapons were permitted. God created men and women perfectly from the very best mould, but people rebel and sin. Therefore, those who sin will be reduced to the lowest status of all. Those who believe and act righteously will be raised to the highest status, above the angels.

Surah 106 proclaims that "The Quraysh" (who give the *surah* its name) are a noble people. They enjoy many covenants of peace and security in Arabia but fail to adore God, who provides for their every need, feeding them, clothing them, sheltering them and protecting them from danger. A possibly posthumous *hadith* restricts the caliphate to the Quraysh as long as a single clan member lives (Bukhari, 89: 253).

Surah 101, "The Calamity" describes the Day of Judgement as a calamity when men will be scattered like moths and the mountains turned into string that can be woven like wool. Those whose good deeds weigh heavier than their bad deeds will enter paradise, but those whose bad deeds outweigh their good deeds will enter the Fire.

Surah 75, "The Resurrection", says that the Day of Judgement is also the day of resurrection when the dead will be raised and judged. Sceptics demand to know when the day of resurrection is, so that they can continue to do wrong then repent in time for judgement. Muhammad is again instructed not to hasten recitation. On that day, some faces will brighten as they look towards the Lord (see also 83: 35).

According to 104, "The Scandalmonger", those who selfishly store up wealth, or engage in backbiting and gossip, merely prepare their place in hell.

Surah 77, "The Sent", begins with a divine oath, "By the winds sent forth". Every few verses of this chapter's 50 warn those who reject Truth, who refuse to pray and who treat others unjustly, of the judgement to come. A poetic chapter, the wicked are warned that on that day they will be unable to defend themselves, since their actions, not their words, will speak for them. On that day, they will find neither shade nor respite. It will be too late to believe in the Message that was sent to them.

Surah 50 is named after the opening cryptic letter, "*Qaf*". The Qur'an is again described as "glorious". People are mistaken to think they will die and rise again to eternal life when they live wicked lives. Some deliberately misunderstand Muhammad's message. They fail to see God's hand in the perfection of nature, just as earlier people failed to listen to their prophets. Noah is mentioned in verse 12 (the first reference so far). The people of 'Ad, the Thamud, Pharaoh and the companions of Rass (whose identity is uncertain) all rejected their messengers. Verse 16 says that our Creator is nearer to us than our jugular vein, that is, God sees deeply into our souls. Verse 17 refers to the two angels, one on our right and one on our left, who record respectively our good and bad deeds. When the final trumpet blows, the angels will bear witness to our deeds. If we did what was wrong, worshipped a false God or ignored the truth, hell waits for us. If we sincerely turned to God and did what was right, the Garden waits for us. Verse 38 refers to God creating the earth in six days without becoming tired. God is patient, waiting for people to turn towards God in praise and prayer. Night is best for prayer, before dawn. Muhammad is commanded to warn people of what is to come "with the Qur'an".

Surah 90, "The City", celebrates Muhammad's special relationship with Mecca. He is described as a "freeman" of the city. The arrogant who think they have no need of God are denounced. The righteous are those that choose a "steep path", which consists of freeing slaves, feeding the hungry, caring for orphans and the homeless, kindness and compassion. These are those of the "right hand". Those of the "left" reject God's signs, for them the Fire is waiting, surrounded by a wall too high to scale.

Surah 86, "The Night Stars", begins with a divine oath, "By the stars". Man may be physically unimpressive but his soul is magnificent, God's special gift. Verses 6–7 identify our loins as the locus of our being. From this point, our form, personality and spirit grew from the clot, or "drop" with which God gifted us life. After death, God can restore our personhood. Verse 17 is a generous promise that even the lives of unbelievers will be extended to allow them yet another opportunity to repent.

Surah 54, "The Moon", says that too many people would even ignore a sign of the impending Judgement if it was announced by the moon splitting in two. They would call this magic and continue to follow their lust. Again, Muhammad's listeners are reminded how earlier people rejected their prophets. Noah's story is told in more detail. He warned the people (which is not part of the biblical narrative; Genesis 6–9). They refused to listen. So God sent a great flood. Noah was prepared for this, having built a boat. Those who saw it floating on the waters had left their repentance too late. The 'Ad, too, were warned but did not listen. A great wind destroyed their city. Verse 22 is the first reference so far to the Qur'an as "easy to understand". It is a clear, plain, easy warning that nobody ought to ignore. Verses 32 and 40 repeat this description, which is a major motif. The people of Thamud also spurned their prophet, Salih, lampooning him as a solitary madman. Why should they follow him? Calling him an insolent liar, they refused to allow the she-camel to drink her fill, ham-stringing her instead (see 91 above). The charge here is that while water and pasture should have been common property, the elite monopolized these resources. For this, God sent a great wind to destroy their city. The people of Lot also ignored their warning, so a tornado destroyed them. Lot himself was saved. Pharaoh, too, rejected God's signs. The Quraysh may think they are better than these earlier peoples, that they possess immunity or can defend themselves even against God. The wicked are among the insane, not God's messengers or those who embrace God. Destroying the Quraysh is as easy for God as winking his eye, for by such an act he formed the world in all its proportions. All that the wicked and the good do is recorded in their Books; Gardens and Rivers wait for the latter, but the former will have no excuse, for even their smallest deeds have been written down. According to tradition, the moon did split into two "during the lifetime of Allah's apostle" (Bukhari, 58: 208–11). *Hadith* 208 says that Muhammad pointed to the moon splitting when the sceptics demanded a miracle. Surah 2: 23 implies that the Qur'an was the only miracle to which Muhammad could point as confirmation of his mission.

Surah 38 is named after the opening cryptic letter, "*Sad*". Muhammad is accused of sorcery and of lying, but the Qur'an is a book of Truth. The Qur'an is a "*dhikr*". The word *dhikr* (remembrance) is also used for meditative repetition of God's names. It conveys the meanings of warning and of teaching, so that people are reminded again and again of God's will and way. Arabs seem surprised that God has sent a prophet from their own people. Yet they reject God's messenger, as if it were they who ruled the heavens and the earth. Noah's people, the 'Ad, the Thamud, Lot's people, Pharaoh and others all rejected their prophets, and were destroyed. We meet David and Solomon for the first time in this chapter. The interest here is in their dual roles as prophets and kings. Later, Muhammad combined spiritual and political authority. David adjudicates a dispute between two brothers, and does so justly. David is described as a *Khalif* (Caliph), or Viceroy (as we shall see, humanity is also a *Khalif*). Muhammad's political successors were *Khalifs*. As *Khalif*, David must rule and judge justly. Nowhere does the Qur'an mention David's act of adultery. God gifted David with his son, Solomon, who was tempted by worldly power and success but who repented and turned towards God in true devotion. We also encounter Job for the first time. Job was tested by Satan and complained about his suffering. God restored his fortune twofold. Abraham, Isaac, Jacob, Ishmael, Elisha and Dhu al Kifl (perhaps Ezekiel, or a non-biblical prophet) are listed as of the company of the good. Eternal gardens await the righteous; eternal fire the wicked. This is the first detailed description of paradise; there will be abundant fruit and delicious drinks. Virgins (verse 52) are promised. Non-Muslims have often remarked on the physicality of Qur'anic descriptions of heaven and hell, suggesting that the promise of virgins and of luxuries in the former was a device to attract converts, especially men. Muslims regard both descriptions as allegory, expressing reward and punishment in language that readily communicates the seriousness of the choice people must make. Many Muslims take these to be the wives of righteous men, awaiting them in paradise, implied by 43: 70. Thus, husbands and wives will be reunited. Muhammad is again described as a "warner", proclaiming the Oneness of God. The warning is plain, and public. Verses 71 to 88 recount the creation of Man and Woman (see also 2: 30–9; 7: 11–25; 15: 26–44; 17: 61–3; 18: 50; 20: 116–24). God announces to the angels that he is to fashion Man from clay, breathe God's spirit into him (as in Genesis). The angels were commanded to prostrate themselves before Man. Iblis refused, and was cursed. Created from fire (15: 27), he was too proud to humble himself before a creature made from clay. He was, however, allowed to live until Judgement Day, permitted to try to corrupt others to follow his evil ways. Iblis is a *jinn*, not an angel, but had inserted himself among them. Angels in Islam do not possess free will; Jinns do. Adam's wife is not mentioned in this passage, she appears in our next chapter. The Qur'an uses the words *insan* (man) and *bashar* (human being) interchangeably, so "the term 'man' can be taken to mean 'humanity' in general, of which Adam is the progenitor" (Sherif, 70).

Surah 7, with 206 verses, is easily the longest so far. It begins with four cryptic letters. Muhammad's hearers should listen to the lessons of the past. The Book he is receiving intends to lift all burdens and difficulties. God made us and shaped us. Here, the Qur'an addressed men and women as "you". All the angels except Iblis bowed down before us. When challenged why he disobeyed, Iblis said that as a creature made from fire he was superior to creatures made of clay. Iblis, given respite until Judgement Day, pledges to tempt people from the "straight path". Verse 19 commands Adam and his wife (thus, they were created as a pair) to dwell in paradise, where they can eat any fruit except one, which was forbidden. Iblis tempted them to eat that fruit and they did. God then banished them from paradise. This story continues in Surah 2. Verse 46 gives the *surah*'s title, "The Heights". On the Day of Reckoning, a hijab (veil) separates the redeemed from the condemned while a third party sit on the Heights, so can see both heaven and hell. Some commentators identify the people on the Heights as those whose good and bad deeds equally balance, who await God's final decision. Al-Ghazali prefers to see them as the most pious of all, who look "with grace and amity towards those in paradise" but "with scorn at those in the Hell-fire" (Ghazali and Shamis, vol. 1, p. 130). Since Muhammad is "unlettered" (*ummi*), he cannot be accused of writing the Qur'an (verse 157; see 62: 2). Muhammad's illiteracy has been challenged on the basis that he was a successful businessman who also may have written part of at least one treaty (Esack 2005, 102). Others say that he could write but not well, or that he could write but could not have composed the Qur'an because he was unfamiliar with the stories contained in the Book. For many Muslims, belief in Muhammad's illiteracy is almost theological, ensuring that God's word passed unpolluted through him into the world. When Moses asked to see God, he was not permitted to do so but he was allowed to see a reflection of God's glory (verse 143; compare with Exodus 33: 22–3), which caused him to swoon. God communicates to prophets from behind a veil (hijab), usually "through a messenger" (Saeed 2006, 32). *Hijab* appears seven times in the Qur'an (7: 46; 17: 45; 19: 17; 33: 53; 38: 32; 41: 5; 42: 51). Verse 180 refers to God's Beautiful Names; see also 17: 110; 20: 8; 59: 24.

In Surah 72, "Jinn", we learn more about the creatures known as *jinn*, having already met one in the person of Iblis. With 72 verses, this is much shorter. The *jinn*, who have free will, can choose good or evil. Some listened to the Qur'an and embraced its message. This may refer to an incident in 620 CE when Muhammad was returning to Mecca from Al-Taif and stopped on route to pray and recite the Qur'an (Esack 2005, 18). Even while the Quraysh were persecuting Muhammad, these *jinn* were aiding him from the spirit-world. Other *jinn* still oppose the good, having allied themselves with Iblis.

The content of Surah 36, named after the first two "cryptic letters", "*ya sin*", has been described as the "heart of the Qur'an" (Ali, 1116). The Qur'an, which is full of wisdom, points to the straight path. A city thought to be Antioch rejected God's message and was destroyed. Three messengers were spurned because they were foreigners. Why, the people asked, does God not speak to us directly? Some Quraysh leaders rejected Muhammad because they thought God should speak directly to them. Verse 36 refers to God as creating all that is "in pairs" (night, dark, odd, even, male and female). Duality is itself a mercy. Again, this affirms that male and female are equal. Verse 41 describes Noah's ark as a "sign" of divine mercy because it rescued the human race from the deluge. On Judgement Day, not a single soul will be wronged because accurate records are kept. Then, the good will sit in the shade of trees, recline on thrones, enjoy fruit and know eternal peace. Those Satan led astray, despite their ability to reject him, will be judged by their deeds. Their lips will be sealed, since words can not save them. Verse 69 affirms that Muhammad is no poet but the recipient of a clear divine message. No other God will be able to help the wicked. No words of self-defence will be accepted. Verse 77 says that humanity was created from *nutfah*; the "clot of blood" and "*nutfah*" maybe interchangeable.

Surah 25, "The Criterion", is significant in terms of Qur'anic self-understanding; it is "the criterion" between right and wrong. The night–day metaphor contrasts ignorance with knowledge. Verses 2 echoes Surah 112 – God neither begets nor was begotten nor has a partner, suggesting that Christians may have been among the audience. All other Gods are false, created not creators. Verse 5 reflects criticism that Muhammad was preaching ancient tales that he had learned, or that someone taught him. Others demanded that if Muhammad's message was true, God should send an angel directly to them. Angels are creatures of light, according to Islamic tradition, so even if an angel did appear to them, just as Gabriel took a human form to appear to Muhammad, an angel would need to appear in another form to Muhammad's opponents. In verse 8, Muhammad is accused of being bewitched. Paradise is again described as a place of rest and repose. Why, some ask, is the Qur'an not sent down all at once? It is revealed, says verse 32, in stages so that hearts can be strengthened. Moses, assisted by his brother, Aaron, was also given a Book. Noah, the people of 'Ad, Thamud and the companions of Rass, all had their signs and parables but mocked God's messengers, taking their own lusts as their gods. God has sent messengers to every nation, and might have sent a messenger to every city. Verse 54 describes "marriage" (the first reference so far) as having been established by God. Verse 58 again says that God created all that is in six days. The good are those who give generously, who refrain from killing except for a just cause (verse 68), who do not fornicate or worship any God besides Allah. Yet there is still time for the wicked to repent. Reference to killing for a just cause may suggest a later date for this verse, since passages on fighting are generally accepted as Medinan. Verse 52 says "strive (*jihad*) against unbelievers" with God's word, which implies using the beauty, power and persuasive eloquence of the Qur'an to win people to the faith which, says Ali, is the "best *jihad* of all" (see Ali, 901). We return to the word *jihad*, which is used here, later in this book.

In Surah 35, "The Creator", verse 1 refers to creation *ex nihilo*. This chapter stresses God's mercy. Satan can only invite people to enter the Fire. The evil try to make their conduct appear good but they cannot fool God. Verse 11 repeats the affirmation that God created man and woman as a "pair" from "*nutfah*" (a drop of fluid). God determines when we are born and when we die. Just as the sun's and moon's movement are determined by God, so are our days. We need God. God is free from all needs but is worthy of our praise. If God willed, he could destroy this creation and start a new one. Verse 18 invokes regular prayer and purification (a simile for charity). The night–day motif again differentiates ignorance from wisdom. Muhammad has come with clear signs and a Book of Enlightenment. In the past, people rejected their messengers. Prayer, charity and reciting the Book are encouraged. The Book confirms previous Books. The faithful will enter the Garden, where they will find gold ornaments waiting for them. Those who fail to listen to their warner will be punished in the Fire of Hell. No false god, or partner of God, will be able to help them. They had a clear Book but rejected it. Yet Allah in his mercy extends our life-span so that more of us have a chance to repent. Some scholars identify this as the first Medinan *surah*.

Surah 56 is named "The Inevitable", which describes the Day of Judgement, when many will be exalted and many brought low. Some will become companions of the Right hand, some of the Left. The faithful will ascend golden thrones, where they will be surrounded by youths of great beauty, who will serve them wine from which no one will ever become intoxicated. Critics seize on this reference to claim that what Islam prohibits on earth is to be allowed in heaven, which they say is a contradiction. However, no one on earth can drink alcohol over long periods without getting drunk. Many Muslims see these descriptions as allegorical, describing what we cannot yet fully understand because we have yet to enter paradise. In paradise, nobody will behave frivolously. All will greet each other with "*salam*", which is how Muslims greet each other. At verse 91 as at 13: 24 where the angels use the formula, *aSalamu alaykum* (peace be on you) and at 6: 54 we have the actual words Muslims exchange in greeting. Verses also refer to virgin companions, who will be of "goodly number". The wicked will find themselves in a place full of smoke and boiling water. When alive, they enjoyed luxury and scorned the idea that punishment would follow death, thinking that nothing could hurt their "dust and bones". They scorned the possibility that God might resurrect their flesh-and-blood bodies. They will thirst but nothing will quench them. Finally, the Qur'an is described as "most honourable" and "well guarded". It should only be touched by those who are clean – the first reference to the custom of washing hands before handling the Qur'an.

Analysis of the Chapters

The *surahs* discussed in this chapter stress the universal nature of Muhammad's mission, although he is also an Arab prophet with an Arabic scripture. He preached worship of One God, the rejection of other gods, of "idols", of partners in the Godhead. He encouraged charity, care of the needy, prayer and recitation of the Qur'an. The Qur'an is a clear, easy to understand message warning people to turn towards God. Yet God's mercy is stressed. Repentance is always an option while we live but once we are dead our deeds, not any words, will seal our fate. Eternal punishment awaits the wicked, eternal bliss the good. The very physical descriptions of heaven and hell can be understood as allegory. They can also be understood more factually; Islam does not see the physical as less valuable than the spiritual. The concept of *tawhid* (expressed at Surah 112) is about holding different spheres in balance: work and leisure, the material and the spiritual, religion (*din*) and the world (*dunya*). God will resurrect us bodily. Within marriage, sex and sexual pleasure is wholesome. If sex has any place in heaven, it will also be holy and wholesome. Some of the chapters reviewed are known as "*surahs* of wrath" according to a tradition traced from Muhammad (Sherif, 12). Yet the contention that the Qur'an is all about God's anger and the threat of hell misrepresents what has been described. Graphic descriptions of hell are always offset by the promise of repose in heaven and by the possibility of repentance. Throughout, God is depicted as compassionate, merciful. People are reminded of the fate of the unregenerate, but the intent is for them to turn towards God.

All of these chapters have opposition to Muhammad's preaching in the background. Ethical conduct is described in universal language. As yet, although Muhammad is leading a dissident religious movement, no distinctive features have emerged in terms of worship and practice. Muhammad is, however, especially targeted for criticism for endangering the unity of the clan (Lings, 84); he was accused of apostasy from the clan's religion, of splitting "up the Quraysh" and of mocking "their traditions" (Guillaume, 156). Significantly, maintaining the unity of the Muslim community would become a dominant concern, linked with the very notion of *tawhid*; God is one, God's people should also be "one". Reference to David and Solomon as prophet-rulers may point towards Muhammad's future role. The believers, though, do not as yet constitute a "state". Nothing that could be called "law" has been revealed. No "penalties" have been prescribed. Some Muslims did backslide in the face of persecution but many suffered hardship with dignity, remaining faithful. Muhammad, whose role was to warn, did so with courage and patience (except for the occasion when he "frowned"). Although often banned from the area around the Ka'bah, he was allowed to enter during the Sacred Months, when there was a general amnesty (Lings, 89). There were four Sacred Months, when pilgrims came to Mecca. It was at the Ka'bah that several of the *surahs* to which we now turn were proclaimed.

The Qur'an on God, Humanity and Itself 2

The Ethiopian Refugees

Surahs summarized in Chapter 1 already touched on the Qur'an's understanding of itself, of God and of humanity, but these themes develop even more substance in the *surahs* discussed below. This chapter begins with 19, 18, 53 and 20, which I have taken out of Zarkarsh's sequence to better deal with context. During 614, Muhammad sent the first contingent of refugees to seek asylum in Ethiopia (Abyssinia), where they were graciously received by the Negus, or king. Later, the Quraysh sent emissaries to persuade the Negus to hand these apostates over to their custody. Having offered them sanctuary, the Negus was not prepared to breach the rules of hospitality without first hearing from the refugees about their beliefs. Assembling his bishops, he summoned them. The believers recited, or perhaps read to him Surah 19 ("Mary"), which was presumably translated for him into Amharic. This may be the earliest incident of part of the Qur'an being rendered into another language. When the believers recited, "And make mention of Mary in the Book" followed by the annunciation of Jesus' birth, the "Negus wept, and his bishops wept also" and said, "this has truly come from the same source as that which Jesus brought" (Lings, 83). The emissaries then tried to create a rift between the refugees and the Negus by raising the issue of what the former said about Jesus. They presumably hoped that the Negus would find the view of Jesus as only a prophet inadequate. The refugees reply resembles Surah 4: 171, that Jesus was a messenger, a Word and a Spirit from God. The Negus declared that the refugees would remain under his protection. The emissaries went back "to Mecca with the news that they had been rebuffed" (Lings, 85).

Mary: Our First Gospel Narrative

In Surah 19, we encounter Gospel-related narrative for the first time, beginning with the annunciation of the births of John the Baptist and of Jesus. The former is repeated at 3: 38–41, the latter at 3: 42–63. See Luke 1: 11–80 for the Gospel account. The Qur'an's account follows the Gospels' closely, with several exceptions. In verse 9, responding to Zakariya's question, "How could he and his wife have a son in old age?" the Qur'an replies that this is as easy for God as it is to say, "So, it will be," affirming Jesus' virgin birth. Verse 21 repeats this in answer to Mary's question, how would she conceive when no man had touched her? In the Qur'an, God created the universe by saying *Kun* (be) an expression that occurs seven times in the Qur'an; in the Bible God does so by speaking; see Genesis 1: 3, "God said" and Surah 3: 59. Verse 12 refers to John's Book. Thus, John was also a prophet who received a scripture. Verse 23 describes Mary's pain in giving birth, which is not found in the Gospels. She also withdraws to a far place when she gave birth under a palm tree. The far place could be Bethlehem, although Bethlehem is not mentioned by name in the Qur'an. In verse 30, Jesus speaks from the cradle – reminiscent of the Buddha walking and talking at birth. Verses 15 and 33 salute John and Jesus with the peace – blessing the day they were born, the day that they died and the day they are raised up again. Jesus' death, from the Qur'an's point of view, will be discussed when dealing with Surah 4: 157. Mary is the only woman mentioned by name in the Qur'an, rather than as the wife of somebody or as the Queen of somewhere, although she is also described as Jesus' mother, as Imran's daughter and Aaron's sister (Sherif, 90). She is the most frequently mentioned woman (34 times); she is mentioned 19 times in the New Testament (Parrinder, 60). Only seven other people have a chapter named after them.

Non-Muslims have often assumed that Muhammad's contact with Christians in Arabia was the source for this material. Their information was either derived from apocryphal sources or was somewhat garbled, due to lack of contact with the wider Christian world. Parrinder identifies a scribal note to the Arab Infancy Gospel as a possible source for Jesus speaking from the cradle (Parrinder, 78). From a Muslim perspective, the attempt to identify sources is irrelevant; Muhammad recited words as he received them from Gabriel, who brought him God's word. Similarity between passages in the Qur'an and earlier scriptures is due to their common divine origin, not because Muhammad borrowed from them. Criticism that Muhammad preached what others taught him was referred to in Chapter 1. With reference to content related to Christian narrative, he was specifically accused of learning from a Christian slave called Jabr. Surah 16: 103 says, "We know that they say that he is taught by a man but that man's language is foreign while this Qur'an is in pure, clear Arabic" (see Guillaume, 180).

The remainder of Surah 19 divides into four sections, reciting stories linked with Abraham, several prophets including Moses and with the resurrection and judgement. The Abraham narrative here is extra-biblical; scholars suppose that many Abraham-related stories existed in Arabia, where Abraham was regarded as an Arab patriarch. Arabized versions of biblical stories, claiming ownership or rooting events within Arabia, did exist. Again, from the Muslim perspective this is irrelevant, since Muhammad was neither consulting any sources nor composing his Book, but preaching what was word for word God's speech. In Genesis 12: 1, Abraham is told to leave his father's country and journey to the "promised land". Rather as the Talmud adds details to biblical stories, so does the Qur'an. Muslim commentators, says Ali, drew on this material rather too liberally, in his opinion (xv). We learn about how Abraham rejected his father's gods, choosing instead to worship One God. Abraham tells his father to desist from worshipping Satan, since worship of false gods leads to the Pit. Abraham prays that God will bless his father and forgive him, despite his persistence in unbelief. Verse 46 implies that Abraham was banished; his father tells him to "get away from me". Elsewhere, Abraham smashed the idols except for the largest. When blamed for this he jests that perhaps the chief idol had done this, so they should ask him! (21: 63). The Qur'an is clearly interested in hearers drawing analogy between Abraham and Muhammad, who also rejected his father's gods and was "chased out of the city because of his preaching" (Sultan 2004, 75). Later, Muhammad also smashes idols when Mecca was taken in 630 CE. The Moses narrative is related to the event described biblically at Exodus 3 and is repeated in more detail at Surah 20: 9–36. This was Moses' call at the burning bush when Aaron was also appointed as his aide. Verse 54 describes Ishmael as a prophet.

The Qur'an does not share the more negative portrayal of Ishmael at Genesis 17: 12 "he will be a wild man at enmity with all people"; there is no breach between Abraham and Ishmael. Ishmael encouraged his people to pray and to practise charity. Idris, possibly Enoch, a prophet mentioned twice in the Qur'an, was a sincere messenger whom God exalted to high station, which might refer to Genesis 5: 24, where God raised him to heaven. Noah was another prophet on whom God bestowed grace and favour. All prophets were gifted with signs so that those who heed them repent and turn to God will have paradise as their eternal resting-place. As in earlier passages, the Garden is described as a place of peace where no frivolity and vain conversation takes place. In verse 64, the angels explain that they only descend to earth with God's word when commanded to do so. People must be patient; if God is silent it is because of God's inscrutable wisdom, yet signs of God's majesty are all around us. People express scepticism about the resurrection, yet the God who created us can surely also resurrect us from the dead. Have no doubt, says verse 68, that God will gather both the good and the bad before God's throne. None can escape judgement. Those who fail to recognize God's clear signs will have no excuse. Wealth accumulated on earth by those who fail to acknowledge God as owner of all that is will offer no comfort on Judgement Day. Indeed, punishment often begins in this life as gluttony results in ill health, for example (Ali, 759). Finally, people are dissuaded from acting against unbelievers; their days are numbered and God will act when the time is right. On the Day of Judgement, they will be driven like thirsty cattle to hell, where no refreshment or intercession awaits them. The few whom God permits to intercede for others will not do so for the wicked. Certainly, no "son of God" has any such mandate. Calling on God's son to intercede is preposterous presumption. Verse 96, promising resurrection and paradise to the righteous, pronounces that on these women and men God bestows God's love (*hubb*). This expression, in various forms, occurs 69 times in the Qur'an. This is its first appearance, so far, in our paraphrase.

The Satanic Verses Affair

During the Sacred Months, Muhammad was able to preach in the area around the Ka'bah. His preaching involved dialogue as he responded to the criticism and challenges of the Quraysh. Surah 18, "The Cave", appears to have been revealed against this background; Ibn Ishaq describes how the Quraysh offered Muhammad money, or a position of leadership if he would desist from his mission (Ibn Ishaq, 133). According to Ibn Ishaq, the Quraysh said they would believe Muhammad if God would send them an angel to "confirm what he said and to contradict them" (134; and see Surah 25: 7 discussed in Chapter 1). It was at this time that Abu Jahl tried to attack Muhammad with a stone. Shortly after, the *surah* of the cave was revealed. In this chapter of 110 verses, Muhammad is extolled as bringer of the Book that makes the path straight, without any crookedness. He warns those who teach that Allah has a son that this is false. Christians may be the intended audience, although some Arab deities also had sons and daughters. At least in part, what follows appears to have been a response to what Ali describes as "posers" put to the Prophet "which they thought the prophet would be unable to answer" in order to "discredit him" (709). They asked him about the story of the Seven Sleepers of Ephesus. This refers to seven Christians from Ephesus who sealed themselves in a cave (hence the *surah*'s name) to escape persecution. Al-Ghazali, though, says that they "embraced *tawhid*" (Ghazali and Shamis, vol. 2, p. 103). They then slept for centuries. When one of them emerged from the cave, he found a changed world in which Christianity was now popular. The questioners wanted to catch out Muhammad regarding how long the youth had slept in the cave. In the story, the youths thought they had slept for one night. Verse 25 says that they slept for 300 years, but that some add nine more. In telling the story, the Qur'an takes the opportunity to rebuke the questioners for wasting time debating the details of the story, when what is really important is the underlying spiritual message.

This message involves understanding the difference between human time and divine time; the lives of the seven is "a mystery that can be fathomed by the few" (Ali, 706). People argue over how many youths there were, three, four, five and a dog as the sixth. Do not, says the Qur'an, enter into controversy over this; rather, emulate the youths' faith, patience and virtue. Verse 23 echoes the story of the orchard told in Surah 68, warning never to plan tomorrow's agenda without adding "*insha Allah*". Another parable follows, in which two men tend grapevines which yield abundant harvest. God caused a river to flow between the two vineyards. The two men begin to argue. One claimed to be richer. He also claimed that no God could punish him. He "thought he would last for ever" (Ali, 718). The other man acknowledged that Allah was the source of his wealth, responsible for the productivity of his vineyard. Perhaps God would even give him a better gift than the vineyard. Perhaps God might destroy his neighbour's because of his pride. Indeed, the arrogant man's vineyard was laid to waste. Then, he regretted having dishonoured God (possibly by associating partners with God). When the Day of Judgement comes, we will all face our reckoning naked, with nothing to protect us except our deeds and divine justice itself. The Book of Deeds will be placed before us, yet no one will be dealt with unjustly. Verse 50 returns to how God commanded the angels to bow down before Adam and how the jinn Iblis, who had inserted himself among the angels, refused. At the judgement, Iblis will be of no help to those whom he corrupted. Nor will any other intermediary be able to intercede for us, certainly not any divine partner.

The Quran, says verse 54, clearly explains parables and stories for the edification and instruction of people, offering guidance. God's messengers only bring good news, yet unbelievers dispute with them, treating God's signs as if they were in jest. Were God to judge such people immediately, they would be damned, but in God's mercy God extends their time. Beyond this, though, there is no refuge. Many wicked peoples have been destroyed for failing to turn towards God. Moses, who was well schooled in Egyptian learning, went on a quest to acquire more knowledge. During the years of wandering in the wilderness, however, he found that only God could teach him the wisdom he still needed to know. In the following story, another non-biblical narrative, God instructed Moses to find a certain teacher, taking with him a fish (symbolizing knowledge). When he reached the juncture of the two seas, he realized that he had lost the fish. His helper, who was accompanying him, had seen the fish escape but forgot to tell Moses. Wherever the fish disappeared was supposed to mark the place where Moses would encounter the teacher. Not knowing where the fish had escaped, they turned back. As they walked, they became very tired. They struggled on and on. In the end, they did encounter one of God's servants, entrusted with deep and profound knowledge. Tradition calls this teacher Khidr (Ali, 727). Acquiring knowledge is not always easy. It demands patience. Moses now travels with this teacher, agreeing not to ask any questions until the teacher is ready. As they travel, the teacher scuttles a boat then slays a young man. Each time, Moses asks him why he has acted in this way. The teacher rebukes him for breaking his promise. Arriving at a town, they beg food but are refused. After the teacher rebuilt a collapsed wall, he said it was time for Moses to go his separate way, explaining that the boat would have been seized by a king who was appropriating vessels for war. The king would not seize a scuttled boat, so the men who owned it could repair it and resume their livelihoods. The slain youth was rebellious against God, who had decided to gift his parents with a "son better in purity". By restoring the wall, he exposed treasure covered by debris to which two poor orphans were entitled. Moses learned through this not only the lesson of patience but also that when God acts, the purposes of God's acts may not be obvious. Next, Surah 19 tells the story of Dhu al-Qarnayn, commonly identified with Alexander the Great (Sherif, 96). Al-Qarnayn is a powerful king, whose rule stretched from East to West. Mindful of the weak, he governed justly. His power, says the Qur'an, was from God. Once, when he encountered a primitive but peaceful people, he decided to leave them alone and blocked off a mountain gap between their territory and that of their enemies, the Gog and Magog, who constantly attacked them. He took no tribute in return. He then directed their attention to Allah, who is the ultimate protector of all humanity. They should honour Allah. When the trumpet sounds, even the strong barrier he had built for them will be destroyed. Those who scoff now about faith will realize the truth of what they have scorned. Wealth and power in this life will be worthless, if people live selfish, greedy lives. Some people think that by giving to charity with one hand, they can offset the evil they do with their other hand. They will find that what they thought were good works will have no weight at all. Verse 109 eloquently attests that nature is the best sign of God's mercy, so much so that if the oceans of the world were full of ink no volume could exhaust the "words of my Lord". Muhammad was then instructed to declare that he was a man (he claimed no divine status) but that his inspiration came from the One and Only God. All who wish to meet God should live righteously, perform good deeds, worship God and acknowledge that God has no partners.

The issue of God's partners, or of the efficacy of other "gods" to intercede for people, emerges as the dominant theme of Surah 53. Controversy has surrounded this chapter, although this is not due to words found within the chapter itself. It has been generated by the context, or from a passage that some claim was originally part of this chapter before a mistake was corrected. The context is Muhammad preaching at the Ka'bah after the refugees had left for Ethiopia. The background might include some type of Quraysh effort to reach a compromise with Muhammad as described in discussing Surah 109. Surah 53 ("The Star") has 62 verses and divides into three sections. Section one starts with a divine oath after which the chapter is named, "By the stars". It then defends Muhammad from his enemies. He is neither misled nor has he gone astray; he is divinely inspired. In language similar to Surah 81, Gabriel is described as "one mighty in power, endued with wisdom" who takes on "stately form" to bring Muhammad God's word. Muhammad's heart never falsifies what he hears or sees. He may have encountered the charge of fabricating revelation. Certainly, this became a popular accusation in Christian anti-Muslim polemic. Verse 13 may be a reference to an event that has not, according to the standard chronology, happened yet – Muhammad's Night Journey and Ascent (discussed below), described here as the "second descent". The first was the Night of Power. Verses 19 to 23 bring us to the source of controversy, the so-called "Satanic Verses" affair. Presumably actually standing before the Ka'bah and pointing to images, or idols, of three goddesses, Lat, Uzza and Manat, Muhammad denounced these as "nothing but names". We know that he was under pressure to offer some concession to the dominant religion. Many might have eagerly hoped that he would recognize at least some of their gods. Surah 109 could belong here, rather than earlier, in which compromise is rejected. Ibn Ishaq observes that Muhammad's own heart yearned to receive "a message that would reconcile his people to him" (Guillaume, 165). According to Ibn Ishaq, those listening to Muhammad heard him say that the three goddesses were like exalted birds, "whose intercession is approved" (Guillaume, 166). These words, though, came not from Gabriel but from Satan, who, says Surah 22: 52 always tries to substitute false words for the true words of revelation. Gabriel then rebuked Muhammad for this error, and revealed the words that became verses 19–23. Some see this as an example of abrogation, when an earlier verse is cancelled by a later verse although usually both verses remain in the Qur'an. However, the refugees in Ethiopia, hearing that Muhammad was now reconciled with the Quraysh, began to return to Mecca (Guillaume, 167).Verse 38, which says that no one bears the burdens of another, is taken as a repudiation of the doctrine of original sin. Ibn Ishaq locates "He Frowned" (Surah 80) at this point, too, although we discussed this passage in Chapter 1.

The Ban

Critics of Muhammad regard the "Satanic Verses" incident as a compromise, suggesting that if Muhammad was unable to distinguish Satan's words from God's on this occasion, perhaps he was in fact always satanically inspired (Spencer, 82). Muir represents Muhammad as constantly struggling between light and darkness (Muir, 39). Yet such a compromise of Muhammad's strict monotheism and rejection of idols does not sit comfortably with his resolute refusal to contemplate any such concession. Muir thinks that power was all along Muhammad's goal (520), yet if this was the case all he had to do was desist from preaching and accept the wealth and power the Quraysh were offering him (Guillaume, 133–4). Instead, what followed was one of the bleakest periods, as an official boycott of the believers was proclaimed, announced by a notice pinned to the Ka'bah. Since Abu Talib still supported him, his branch of the Quraysh was also included in the ban. Over the next two years, life was even more difficult for Muhammad's companions. Abu Bakr's generosity left him much poorer by the end of the boycott (Lings, 89). He was joined in helping the believers by another powerful Quraysh, who converted towards the end of 616 and the start of 617. The boycott is usually dated from 617 to 619. Umar had opposed Muhammad, whom he accused of splitting the clan, so when his sister became a believer he was furious, resolving to find and kill the Prophet. As he set off on this mission, he was persuaded to first visit his sister to see if he could change her mind. Approaching her home, he overheard the recitation of Surah 20. Bursting in, he demanded that they repeat the babble they had just recited. Initially, fearing his anger, the family refused. Then they handed him a written copy, which he read. Moved by the beauty of what he read, Umar became a believer. Immediately, he decided to find Muhammad so that he could embrace Islam. Seeing Umar, Muhammad assumed that he was still his enemy. Then Umar surprised him by saying that he had come to declare his faith in God (Lings, 86). This incident is often cited as evidence of the power of the Qur'an to touch the most stubborn human heart. This incident also attests to the existence at this stage of written portions.

Surah 20, "Ta Ha", divides into eight sections and is named after the opening cryptic letters. The following identifies the most significant content. The Qur'an is sent down to warn, not to cause distress. The high status of its angelic mediator is again stressed. Verse 8 mentions Allah's beautiful names. God announced, "I am Allah, there is no God but Me," which perhaps corresponds with Exodus 3: 24, "I am Who I Am". God then commands Moses to throw down his staff, which becomes a snake. Al-Ghazali says that verse 18 is a "unique description of Moses' staff not found elsewhere in the Qur'an" (Ghazali and Shamis, vol. 2, p. 123). In the Bible, this happens at Exodus 4: 3. He is instructed to take hold of the snake, since he will remain unharmed. God commands Moses to return to Egypt to challenge Pharaoh, who has "transgressed all bounds". Moses is reluctant, because of his speech-impediment, but God appoints Aaron as his spokesman. The narrative then switches to Moses' birth and rescue from the river, where he had been hidden from Pharaoh who wanted to kill all infant Hebrew boys. This shows how God protected Moses in infancy for the task that lay in his future. Moses and Aaron are advised to reason with Pharaoh, who might be persuaded to set the Hebrew slaves free. Moses addressed Pharaoh in the name of his Lord. Hearing this, Pharaoh jested back that there must be two Lords, since his Lord could not possibly be identical with Moses' Lord. Dialogue followed, in which Moses described his Lord as the One and Only God, who made the earth like a carpet, sends rain and creates all creatures in their pairs. Pharaoh rejects all these signs and accused Moses of intending to drive him out of his own land with magic. This corresponds with Pharaoh demanding a miracle, then summoning his magicians to challenge Moses (Exodus 7: 11). The contest between Moses and the magicians follows (see Exodus 9 for the biblical account); the latter throw down their ropes and sticks, which appear to move like snakes. When Moses threw down his rod, it consumed their "snakes".

The magicians capitulated. Pharaoh accuses his magicians of colluding with Moses, and threatens them with severe punishment. Next, Moses received divine instruction to lead the slaves out of Egypt by night. Surah 20 does not describe the seven plagues (but see 7: 133) or the baking of unleavened bread (Exodus 11: 39), but it does track the fleeing Hebrews to the sea, with Pharaoh's army in hot pursuit. As at Exodus 14: 23 the waters part to allow the Hebrews escape but close up around Pharaoh's army, destroying it. Verse 79 condemns Pharaoh for misrule. He is typically depicted as a tyrant, cruel not only to slaves but also to his own subjects. The Hebrews are fed with manna from above (verse 81; Exodus 17: 12) as God provided for their sustenance in the wilderness. Verses 83 to 89 relate the story of the Golden Calf. While Moses was communicating with God at Mount Sinai, the people back-slid, building an idol of gold (Exodus 32) because Moses was away too long. A man called Samiri, possibly a foreigner, had led them astray (Ali, 781). Complaining that the weight of their ornaments was too heavy, they smelted these down to make an idol. Exodus describes Aaron as supervising the proceedings; 20: 90 depicts him warning the Hebrews that they were being tested by God. Verse 85 says that indeed God had been testing them. At verse 92, Moses reprimands Aaron for not preventing the apostasy. Simiri defends himself by claiming to possess some type of superior spiritual knowledge; he is banished and promised hell as his final destination. Verses 116–24 revisit the creation of Adam and Eve, Iblis' refusal to bow down before them, their eating of the forbidden fruit and exile from paradise. Verse 121 refers to their awareness of nakedness following the act of disobedience and to the sewing together of leaves, as at Genesis 3: 7. Next, the Qur'an departs from the biblical narrative when God "turns towards Adam" – in forgiveness – and grants him Guidance. Adam is recognized as the first prophet. He sinned but was forgiven. Islam does not teach that as a result of the "Fall" all people inherit sin. Islam posits that people have a bias towards forgetfulness but rejects any notion of Original Sin. From the beginning of history, God has given Guidance and sent signs yet people still demand more signs: "Why does he not bring us a sign from his Lord?" Humanity, says verse 132, has had enough signs and messengers for people to choose the straight path (see also 6: 37–9). Verse 113 is the first we have encountered so far that describes the Qur'an as an "Arabic" book, while verse 114 again instructs Muhammad to recite slowly, not to rush revelation which comes as God wills it, although Ibn Ishaq suggests that Muhammad attracted more followers when he recited softly – but not too softly – because people could listen stealthily without attracting the unwelcome attention of his enemies (141).

The Year of Great Sadness

Despite Abu Jahl's protests, the ban was lifted during 619 when it was discovered that the writing on the notice had faded (Guillaume, 172). This was taken as a sign that it ought to be revoked. A period of deep sadness for Muhammad, however, followed the lifting of the ban. In quick succession, Khadijah and Abu Talib both died. The latter did not become a believer but at considerable personal cost had staunchly and loyally defended his nephew. Another *surah* that can be anchored with some confidence is 17, which refers to an event usually dated sometime during 620, as God's response to the Prophet's need for comfort. Before summarizing 17, we visit 26, 27 and 28. Called "The Poets", 26 begins by describing the Qur'an as a clear revelation, yet when people hear a new verse they refuse to listen. They mock at the truth. God's provision of Aaron as Moses' spokesman is again presented as an act of divine grace, followed by another Moses–Pharaoh narrative. This time, Pharaoh tries to divert Moses from his goal of freeing the slaves, reminding Moses that although raised as one of his own royal children, he had slain an Egyptian official yet still has the audacity to seek a favour. Moses admitted his error but despite this said that he was now entrusted with the authority of the Lord of all the Worlds. This infuriated Pharaoah, who rebuked Moses for calling his God "Lord of East and West", since as far as Pharaoh was concerned there was "no God but Pharaoh". As proof of his God's power, Moses throws down his rod; this becomes a snake. Pharaoh dismisses this as sorcery and (as described above) summons his own magicians. The contest follows, with the God of the victor getting all the credit. Again, Moses' rod becomes a snake and consumes the magicians' sticks and rods. Again, Moses and the Hebrews leave at night. Again, the sea divides, allows the slaves to go free then destroys the pursuing army. At verse 63, Moses strikes the sea with his rod as at Exodus 14: 16 (a detail not included at Surah 20: 77).

Abraham's departure from the polytheism of his father follows, similar to the narrative at 19: 41–50. Again, Abraham prays for his father's soul, "Oh but that he might avoid the fate of Iblis and all his hosts!" Verses 105 to 122 revisit Noah, his warning, the people's rejection, the story of the flood and of Noah's ark. This is filled "with all creatures", a detail not mentioned at 56: 14. Hud is named as the prophet of the people of 'Ad, who refused to listen, as the people of Thamud refused to listen to their messengers. Such people want to enjoy their wealth, their gardens and their leisure but only those who turn in repentance and faith towards God have this assurance. The example of the she-camel kept away from her pasture, then crippled to dishonour the prophet who taught God's love and concern for all creatures, surfaces again at verses 155–7. Lot's story is retold (verses 160–75), including Lot's wife perishing with the damned because she hung or looked back instead of fleeing in haste (see Genesis 19: 26). Verses 176 to 191 refer to the Companions of the Wood, who might have been the Midianites. They rejected their prophet, named as Shu'ayb, who has been identified with Jethro. Ali rejects this, saying that "Shu'ayb belongs to Arab rather than to Jewish traditions" (Ali, 368 n. 1054). Calling him bewitched, a "mortal like us" and a liar, they refused to listen. Their city was destroyed. Verses 192 to 227 develop the theme of the Qur'an speaking about the Qur'an. While *surahs* reviewed in Chapter 1 stressed the universal nature of its message, there is emphasis here on the Arabic nature of the revelation. It is written in transparent, clear or perspicuous Arabic. There is a hint here that God chose Arabic because it is the most exalted, precise and eloquent of tongues. Certainly, if Muhammad had recited the Qur'an in any non-Arab language, no Arab would have listened. Yet God is always just. God has never condemned or destroyed any people without first sending a prophet. The title of this *surah* derives from verse 224, which describes the poets as leading people astray. The poets here include enemies of Muhammad, who used poetry to satirize him. The last verse, 227 is probably from Medina, since it refers to those who defend themselves when unjustly attacked. It is generally thought that permission to use self-defence dates from soon after 622. Critics of Muhammad point to the later assassination of several poets after the *hijrah*, arguing that he either encouraged or ordered this. Lings, commenting on the killing of Kab Ibn 'Ashraf, wrote, "it was vital to show … that if hostile thoughts were tolerable, hostile action was not", pointing out that Kab actively mustered troops to attack Medina (Lings, 160, 171). For a negative take on Muhammad and "poets" describing two additional incidents, see Spencer, 162–3.

Surahs 27, "The Ants", and 28, "Stories", contain 93 and 88 verses respectively. They both begin with cryptic letters. Surah 27 reconfirms that the Qur'an is a clear revelation, a guide and a message of hope for believers. Gabriel's high status is also praised. Moses at the Burning Bush, God's command that he throw down his rod and Moses' commission to present signs to Pharaoh, described as nine signs (see Ali, 380), follow. Verses 15–31 speak of David's and Solomon's gift of wisdom. At verse 19, Solomon expressed concern for ants, least they be crushed under foot by his army; even ants have their role in God's economy (18). Wise Solomon knew the speech of birds, so was able to use these as scouts to reconnoitre enemy terrain. One day, he missed the Hoopee bird and was angry that he was absent for muster, but the bird had actually discovered the Queen of Sheba. She ruled over her people, who worshipped the Sun, from a golden throne. Incidentally, there is no hint of censure here concerning her rank as a regnant Queen. Solomon sent the Hoopee back with a letter inviting the Queen and her people to submit to the true religion, to worship the One and Only God. Consulting her advisors, the Queen sent a present to Solomon, but as Solomon was already wealthy, he had no need of any gift. What he wanted was to share his faith with her, not wealth. He asked his chiefs which of them could bring him her throne. A jinn replied that he could. Solomon, however, did not rely on the strength of the jinn to bring him the throne, since such a demonstration of coercive power would compromise his integrity. Rather, another servant used spiritual power to transport the throne. Solomon took this as a sign from God, since the servant had acted without offering to do so, unlike the jinn. Solomon then asked the servant to make the already beautiful throne even more beautiful. When the Queen, invited to Solomon's court, came, he asked her if this was her throne. She said that it was indeed very much like her throne and that she had submitted to Allah as the true God. The moral of this story is that Solomon won her to true faith by spiritual acumen, not by a display of temporal power. Narratives related to the Thamud and Lot follow. Again, Lot's wife fails to escape. Verse 59 invokes peace on all God's servants. Verse 62 says that God listens to the prayers of those who suffer. God guides us through the darkness of land and sea. Despite human ingratitude, God is full of grace towards us. Verse 76 says that the Qur'an explains to the Children of Israel the points "in which they disagree", perhaps referring to dialogue between Muhammad and Jews regarding his and their beliefs. This is our first reference to the Children of Israel. Yet no one can guide the blind and the deaf, that is, people who choose not to see God's signs or to hear God's word. The motif of mountains as apparently fixed in place, but astonishing people when they disappear like passing clouds, introduces the "artistry of Allah, who disposes everything". Rehearse the Qur'an and accept its guidance, we are told, because this leads to the gate of heaven. Those who reject God's word are hell-bound. Our actions alone will condemn or excuse us on the Day of Reckoning. Surah 28 begins by rehearsing some of the story of Moses. Moses' escape from slaughter, shadowed by his sister who called his mother to act as his nurse-maid, the murder of the Egyptian overseer, the flight to Midian where Moses tended Jethro's flocks and married his daughter, are described in the following verses. The title is from verse 25, when Moses narrates the story of his flight from Pharaoh's cruel and unjust rule. In verse 15, he repented of having killed the overseer, attributing this to Satan's mischief. In verse 16 God forgives him.

The burning-bush episode is again narrated, including the command to throw down Moses' rod, which then became a snake, and Aaron's appointment as Moses' aide. By verse 36 Moses is before Pharaoh. Arrogant and insolent, Pharaoh refuses to listen, only to lose his army as the waters close around it. Moses was given his Book. Muhammad, like Moses, has been sent to warn his people, to whom no previous warner had been sent. Had God not sent him, sooner or later the Quraysh would have demanded a prophet. Yet now that Muhammad is among them, they refuse to listen, accusing him of witchcraft. They even demand that he bring them a better Book. They fear that if they follow Muhammad, they will lose the prestige they enjoy throughout Arabia. There, they have established themselves a sanctuary, Mecca, protected by many treaties. God promises that no city is ever destroyed unless it is full of iniquity. They should learn the value of spiritual health, not place all their trust in material wealth. Verse 70 proclaims, "He is Allah, there is no God but He", which summarizes the monotheistic core of all that the Qur'an teaches. Night and Day are signs of God's mercy, since we need one for rest and one for work. From every nation, God has raised up a witness. A saying numbers God's messengers as 124,000, that is, one for every nation. Verse 76 refers to Korah and to his Companions who rebelled against Moses, claiming that their social status entitled them to a more important role (Numbers 16: 1–35). Pride came before a fall; verse 81 says that God caused the earth to swallow them up with all they possessed. Good deeds will attract an even greater reward; evil deeds attract punishment proportionate to the deed, such is God's mercy. The Qur'an is a mercy from God. A reference in verse 85 to Muhammad returning to "the Place" may indicate that this passage was revealed during the migration; verses 52–5 and 85 are identified as from Medina.

The Night Journey and Ascent

Details of this event are narrated in Ibn Ishaq. His account describes how Muhammad, accompanied by Gabriel, was flown on a winged beast, Buraq, then set down on the temple Mount in Jerusalem, where he met Abraham, Moses and Jesus. Muhammad commented on Abraham's physical resemblance to himself. This can be compared with Jesus' meeting Moses and Elijah on the mount of Transfiguration (Mark 9). Both incidents imply a confirming of the prophet's role and status. Gabriel then cleansed his heart before he ascended through the seven heavens to the Throne, where he was instructed to establish 50 daily prayers for his community. As he descended, he again met Moses, who suggested that 50 prayer-times were too much of a burden. As Muhammad went back to ask for fewer prayer-times, this process repeated itself until the five were found acceptable (Guillaume, 186–7). Travelling through the heavens, he also met John the Baptist, Joseph son of Jacob, Idris and other prophets and patriarchs. According to tradition, it was then that Gabriel demonstrated the complete prayer ritual, which implies that Surah 1, "The Opening" (al-fatiha), was revealed before or at this point. Surah 1, which is always recited during ritual prayer, has been described as containing the essence of the Qur'an (Ali, 13). It stresses God's mercy. God is cherisher and sustainer of all, king of the universe. Verse 2 of the Qur'an, then, establishes God's absolute mastery, "everything that has existed or shall ever exist is subordinate to God", who alone is worthy of worship; only God's aid is to be sought (Ghazali and Shamis, vol. 1, p. 12). God guides people along the straight path (siratul mustaqeem). This is the path of those who experience God's grace, not of the wicked.

Surah 17, named after the night journey, has 111 verses. The actual incident is taken by some Muslims to have been a spiritual experience, not a physical event; Ibn Ishaq hints at this when he says, "only God knows how revelation came and he saw what he saw" but "whether he was awake or asleep, it was all true and actually happened" although Muhammad was mocked mercilessly for telling this story (Guillaume, 183). Verse 1 summarizes the incident, referring to Muhammad's night journey to "the farthest mosque". Identified as Jerusalem, this city is considered one of three sacred (haram) places, after Mecca and Medina. Moses and Noah are named as earlier prophets, who presented clear signs to the Children of Israel, who broke their covenant and so were punished. Verse 5 is taken to refer to the Babylonian exile of 586 BCE, while verse 7 is taken as a reference to the Second Temple (from 515

BCE). Verse 9 describes the Qur'an as offering true guidance. The day–night motif follows. All people's deeds are written on a scroll, so there is no escape from our own actions. Guidance is given us for our benefit, so we should listen to God's word. No one can carry our burdens for us (15); Islam does not recognize the concept of a vicarious atonement, unlike Christianity, which teaches that Jesus took our sins upon himself. God, says verse 21, gifts some more than others. Some Muslims have used this and similar verses to justify rule by an elite. Once again, the Qur'an returns to the apparent success and prosperity of the wicked. However, this is also taken to mean that those who possess material wealth may actually be spiritually dead; some who have less wealth may be spiritually much richer. As throughout the Qur'an, Allah is exalted as the only subject worthy of worship. The miserly are siblings of Satan; only the selfless please God. Never murder your children for fear of want, because God will provide. Never take a life except for a just cause, because all life is sacred. Care for orphans. Never cheat customers, but give measure for measure. Do not attempt to substitute the human for the divine, because it is God not women and men who can rend the earth asunder. Verse 40 specifically condemns associating sons and daughters with God. *Shirk* (association) is considered to be an unforgivable sin. The truth is clearly explained in the Qur'an, so no one has any excuse. Verse 44 refers to the seven heavens; Ibn Ishaq's account of the Ascent describes Muhammad passing through each of these. Surahs 23: 84; 41: 12; 65: 12; 67: 3; 71: 15; and 78: 12 all refer to seven heavens. Those who refuse to see God's majesty reflected in nature may well find that they also fail to hear God's clear voice through the Qur'an, as if they are separated from God's word by a barrier, or *hijab* (45). They jest at the idea of the resurrection, claiming that Muhammad is bewitched. Satan is humanity's enemy, not friend. No false God can intercede for the wicked. The she-camel's ill-treatment is again mentioned at verse 59. Verses 61–3 return to Iblis refusing to bow to Adam, who was created from clay. God allows Iblis to tempt women and men with the promise that all who follow him will end up in hell. Over God's true servants, Iblis has no authority or power. Verse 66 introduces the notion that the sea is a mercy from God; God allows us to cross the seas safely in pursuit of commerce and learning. This and other verses suggest that God structured the world to make life easier for us, as a kindness. The spiritually blind in this world will remain blind in the next. Those whose Books record their good deeds have nothing to fear in the afterlife.

Verses 73–80 mention prayer-times. Prayer is to be said as the sun declines and in the small hours of the morning. Verse 82 refers to the gradual descent of the Qur'an as a mercy to believers and a warning to the unjust. Inspiration comes to Muhammad at God's command. Critics would accuse him of somehow stimulating, or fabricating messages of personal convenience to justify his own actions. The Quran explains every kind of parable and metaphor, yet some still demand a miracle before they accept its message. Make the sky split across, they demand, or a spring to gush from the desert. Verse 95 repeats the demand for an angelic messenger instead of Muhammad. Verse 101 refers to the nine signs given to Moses (which were mentioned at 27: 12 and are described at 7: 133). Verse 103 says that Pharaoh and all who were with him were drowned for their faithlessness. The Children of Israel were promised security in their land, conditional on keeping their covenant. Verse 104's reference to their being gathered in a "mixed crowd" (*lafif*) "out of various nations" (Pickthall) might describe the return of Jews to Israel; Dawood has "we shall assemble you all together" (291). The Qur'an is conveniently divided into parts to aid its memorization and recitation, says verse 106. Those who truly know the previous scriptures recognize its truth, and prostrate when they hear it recited. They recognize that promises made earlier have been fulfilled. Muhammad may have expected Christians and Jews to recognize him as the prophet like unto Moses, or as the Paraclete; the Paraclete at John 14: 16 is taken to refer to Muhammad (Guillaume, 103–4). Any one of Allah's most beautiful names may be used in prayer, but no intercession is to be expected from any son, or partner of God. God has none. God requires no helper. Al-Ghazali points out that this *surah* mentions the Qur'an eleven times, which is a unique feature (Ghazali and Shamis, vol. 2, p. 90). Here, the Qur'an is self-conscious of its function and qualities.

Support from Yathrib

During 620, Muhammad married the widow Sawda, who had returned from Ethiopia, and A'aisha, Abu Bakr's daughter, although their marriage was not consummated until some years later. Muhammad then made a lonely journey to the city of Al-Taif to try to attract support. Even Muir expresses praise; "There is something lofty and heroic in this journey of Mohammad to Al-Taif, a solitary man, despised and rejected by his own people, going boldly forth in the name of God, like Jonah to Ninevah, summoning an idolatrous city to repent and support his mission" (113). Sadly, though, the citizens of Al-Taif did not respond. That same year, however, six pilgrims from the oasis of

Yathrib, about 250 miles from Mecca, heard Muhammad preach. Becoming believers, they pledged him their support. The next year, a larger contingent from Yathrib of 75 citizens added their support. These two incidents are known as the first and second pledge of Aqaba. This prepared the ground for Muhammad's migration, the turning-point in Islam's early history. Continuing to follow Zarkashi's sequence, the next three *surahs* follow the numerical, standard order of 10–12. Surah 10 begins with cryptic letters and is named after Jonah (verse 98), which is appropriate given Muir's allusion above. It is the only *surah* that shares a name with a book of the Bible. Jonah's story was part of a very early *surah*, 68. Surah 10 also contains Noah's story (71–4), and part of Moses' (75–92) and again refers to God settling the Children of Israel in security in their Promised Land. Once more, we are reminded that God has sent messengers to every nation and people (verse 47) but that too often human hearts spurn God's word and persecute God's messengers. These people would, if they could, ransom their own souls against the penalty that awaits them but their acts have already damned them. God gives life and takes it back again. Worship of God's partners, a recurring motif, is condemned at verse 66. Those who say that Allah has a son are totally mistaken. We should follow the guidance revealed in the Qur'an. Verse 62 says that those who are Allah's friends (*awliyah*) have no cause to fear. The term "friend" is discussed in Chapter 4. Verse 94 says that if Muhammad had any doubt about the meaning of a revelation he could consult the people to whom previous scriptures had been sent.

Surah 11, which also begins with cryptic letters, is entitled Hud, who, introduced to us in Surah 26, was the prophet of the 'Ad, one of the 25 prophets named in the Qur'an. Content is similar to several *surahs* already summarized. We are reminded that Noah's warning was ignored and that the flood resulted (verses 25–35) with the added detail that one of Noah's sons was left behind (43). He is counted as a wrongdoer. Verses 50 to 60 tell us about Hud, whose people complained that he did not bring clear signs, so they had no intention of forsaking their gods. He invited them to repent, to seek forgiveness. They refused. Hud was saved but the 'Ad were "removed from sight". In verse 61 we again meet Salih, prophet of the Thamud. Verse 64 tells us that the she-camel is a symbol of Allah's bounty. She had the right to feed from Allah's "free earth". We know her fate from earlier *surahs*; she is crippled. The she-camel, I think, is a beautiful example of a Qur'anic parable, although an early Christian polemicist, John of Damascus (d. 749) ridiculed his own completely garbled version without much knowledge of the actual story, calling it one of many "idle tales worthy of laughter" (Sahas, 139–41). The Thamud are destroyed. Verses 70 to 83 contain new material from the life of Abraham. Verses 69–71 refer to the angels who were sent to warn Lot of Sodom and Gomorrah's destruction, and who were entertained by Abraham. God's announcement that, in their old age, Abraham and Sarah would have a son, Isaac, is described at verse 72. At verse 74, Abraham pleads with God on behalf of Lot's people.

The biblical dialogue here (Genesis 18: 25–32) reminds me of Muhammad bargaining down the number of prayer-times; if there are 50 righteous people in the city, would God save them? Would he save them for 40's sake? Finally, would he save them for the sake of ten? Similarly, verse 118 declares that God would not destroy any community for a single wrong act, allowing people time to repent and mend their ways. Shu'ayb, prophet of Midian, features from verse 84 to 95. The command to trade fairly and to give measure for measure is repeated at verse 84. The people of Midian, however, do not want to desist from their ancestral religion. Islam's concern for the honest conduct of business is evident here; if you cheat your customers you cannot then assume that your regular prayers will excuse you. Moses appears again before Pharaoh at verse 96. Moses, says verse 110, was given a Book. God could have made humanity one community, had he willed. Ali comments that the gift of free will made "difference inevitable", which would not matter at all if people turned to God. Unfortunately, selfishness, greed and lust for power corrupt us, causing disputation and conflict.

Surah 12 is called "Joseph", named after the biblical patriarch. It also begins with cryptic letters. The opening paragraph describes the Qur'an as "an Arabic Qur'an" and the story of Joseph as a "most beautiful story". The biblical narrative is Genesis 37 to 50. What follows in Surah 12 is the most sustained narrative we have encountered so far. All 111 verses tell the story, which is offered as a sign. Perhaps the difference between the Qur'an's account and Genesis is that in the former Joseph is described as gifted by God with knowledge and was tempted by Potiphar's wife. The Qur'an implies the gift of knowledge, hence Joseph's ability to interpret dreams, but denies that Joseph experienced temptation. The narrative is eloquently told. Joseph's dying wish is to be counted a Muslim, united with the righteous. Later passages speak of the unity of all the prophets, Muhammad and his predecessors, who all preached the message of Islam. Verse 76 uses the word *daraja* (degree, rank). Several Qur'anic verses refer to God raising some above others in degree, or in knowledge (see 6: 165; 43: 32; 58: 1). Some have argued that such people can claim special authority; others suggest that as people become spiritually rich God blesses them with even deeper understanding.

Surah 15 "Rocky Tract", begins with cryptic letters, followed by the affirmation that the verses of the Qur'an are clear signs pointing the way towards belief in God. The day will come when many unbelievers will regret that they ignored its clear message. God, though, protects and guards God's word. As we shall see, while earlier scriptures may be corrupt, the Qur'an remains pure. Muslims believe that the mechanism through which the Qur'an was collected, codified and eventually printed was free from error, due to divine oversight. The Qur'an is thus guarded from corruption. All messengers have been mocked and ridiculed as mad or possessed. Yet all people are warned before God destroys them for their iniquities. This *surah* emphasizes God's grace through nature, which feeds and sustains us. Verses 26–44 revisit the story of Adam's creation and Iblis' rebellion. This is followed by the promise of paradise for the righteous, who will know no fatigue as they dwell in peace. Our hearts will be purified, so that nothing negative remains at all. Verses 51 to 79 repeat the story of Abraham learning that in his old age he is to have a son, followed by the fate of Sodom. Then we again meet the Companions of the Wood (see 26: 176), who rejected God's signs and were punished. Similarly, the people of the Rocky Tract (verse 80, which names the *surah*) a hill some 150 miles north of Mecca, rejected their messengers. They carved great fortresses from the mountains, but to no avail. God blasted these buildings into oblivion. Ali identifies them as the Thamud (632). Verse 87 refers to the "seven often repeated verses" of the Qur'an, almost certainly Surah 1, *Fatiha*, described above, since this is repeated every prayer-time. Verse 91 refers to how the Quraysh physically abused the Qur'an, tearing it into shreds, which again suggests that some passages existed in written form at an early period. *Shirk* is roundly condemned – associating another god with Allah – but those who prostrate before God in adoration, who serve God faithfully, have no cause to fear the "Hour that is Certain", death.

Surah 6, called "The Cattle", has 165 verses. Such is the length of this late Meccan chapter that it begins to resemble the longer Medina passages. Hearers are invited to travel the earth to learn what fate befell those who rejected God's revelations, despite clear messages and signs. The Qur'an brings blessings and confirms earlier revelations. Again, God's grace and majesty in creation are affirmed. Those who believe in God's signs are to be greeted with *aSalamu Alaykum* (verse 54). God sends rain to water our crops and created all the fruits each with their distinctive flavour, colour and shape.

Cattle can carry our burdens and feed us (142). Implicit here is the invitation to use our intellect to discern signs of God in creation. Verse 19 speaks about Muhammad's inspiration and of God's Oneness; there is One God, not many. This monotheistic motif is sustained throughout the Qur'an. People should prepare for Judgement Day, because those who postpone this can not then say that they would have repented but that death surprised them. Despite their courage and suffering, God's messengers have been scorned. Yet God is merciful. God has inscribed the "rule of mercy" in the Qur'an. All who repent, who refuse to worship false gods, who resist selfish desires, have reservations in paradise. Several verses condemn the killing of children (140, 151). Constantly, the Qur'an stresses God's mercy alongside his justice. Justice demands that the wicked are punished, but it also demands that the good are rewarded. On the one hand, the many references to our actions condemning or excusing us suggest that good works will save us. Indeed, since we do not have to find a remedy for original sin, according to Islam, we are capable of selfless living. On the other hand, the key concepts here are repentance and turning towards God, whose grace then becomes operative in our lives.

Verse 70 reminds hearers that on Judgement Day it will be too late to find an intercessor, or to offer any ransom or excuses for our actions. Take religion seriously now, says this verse. Verses 74–83 revisit Abraham pleading with his father, who once took a star as his God. Verse 84 names many of Muhammad's predecessors, Isaac, Jacob, Noah, David, Solomon, Job, Joseph, Moses, Aaron, who have all had their reward. So too have Jesus, Ishmael, Elisha, Jonah and Lot. All were prophets invested with Books, charged to enlighten a "new people". Muhammad in his turn is entrusted with a message for all nations. His Book, which is full of blessings, confirms previous scriptures. Verse 91 is the first passage encountered so far that suggests that these earlier scriptures are no longer entirely trustworthy; much of their content has been "concealed". This introduces the charge of *tahrif*, the accusation that for their own purposes and to promote their own superior and exclusive religious claims, Jews and Christians tampered with their scriptures. Lying against Allah, they sow seeds of confusion. They choose what they like and ignore the rest. This verse (159) is taken as a warning that Muslims should not endanger the unity of Islam. Those who believe in the Qur'an and pray regularly place their faith in a scripture that is wholly reliable. Here, the Qur'an delineates its position vis-à-vis other scriptures, explaining why such a Book had to be sent, why its message speaks to all humanity. On the other hand, Muslims are to believe in the earlier scripture (2: 4, 136, for example; see Conclusion for further discussion of *tahrif*). Some wicked people even elevate jinns as gods, although they are creatures of God, who created all that is, and who does not have a wife, so God can not give birth either! Verse 118 describes distinctive features of the community Muhammad was now leading. The believers must only eat meat over which God's name has been pronounced, from which the blood has drained (*halal*). Pork is an abomination. Only in an emergency can believers eat meat that has been prohibited (*haram*). Finally, verse 165 describes humanity (as does 2: 30) as a *Khalifa*, God's agent on earth. Surah 33: 72 calls the earth a "trust" (*amanah*) which was first offered to the heavens, the earth and the mountains, but they refused. This reminds me of the Talmudic story of how God offered the Torah simultaneously to 70 nations that all refused before Israel accepted. One day, God will demand an account of how we have exercised this responsibility. The root here is related to *iman* (faith). Did we, like the people of Thamud, deny God's creatures their natural right to share the planet with us, or did we treat them with kindness and respect? Some people may appear to receive greater gifts than others, but this is so that God can test each one of us in our stewardship of what we have received, as with the parable of the talents (Matthew 25: 14–30).

Surah 37, "Those Ranged in Ranks", has 182 verses. The earlier prophets, Noah (75–82), Abraham, Moses and Aaron (114–20), Elijah (122–30) and Lot (133) all succeeded in defeating evil. So too did Jonah (139–46). Here, the plant that gave Jonah shade is described, as at Jonah 4: 6. God's whole creation is designed to ensure evil's defeat. The reference at verse 36 to "a poet possessed" suggests that this was a charge against Muhammad that would not easily go away. Servants of Allah, in their sincerity and devotion, persevere against all odds. Spiritually, however, God aids them even when, in the physical realm, the odds appear stacked against them as men and women reject the Qur'an. "Ranks" occurs in verse 1; the good form rank on rank of people who serve God and God's cause. Surah 34, "Sheba", has 54 verses. God's absolute power is celebrated. David and Solomon are praised for planning and building the Temple. Most of the people of Sheba (verse 15), centuries after Solomon's time, turned away from God. However, a faithful remnant was forgiven when Sheba was destroyed. Verse 34 points out that it is often the rich who are the first to reject God's word, probably because they dislike God's command to give to the needy.

Surahs 31 and 39 can be summarized together. Zarkashi places them before and after 34. Their content, with some beautiful verses, overlaps. 31 is named for Luqman, a figure from Arab tradition, who teaches his son to worship the one true God. 39 takes its name, "crowds" from verse 71 which describes unbelievers as hell-bound in great number, matched by crowds of righteous passing into heaven (73). Allah understands all mysteries. Creator and sustainer of the world, Allah has sent us the Qur'an, a book of wisdom. Nothing and nobody is to be worshipped besides Allah. God created all creatures in pairs, a partner for each of us. Only God can grant the right to intercede. God authored colors and sends rain from the sky. Ships sail the seas by Allah's leave, as night follows day. If the oceans were ink and all trees were pens they could not exhaust Allah's praise (see 18: 109). No one can bear anyone else's burdens. On that day, a trumpet will sound. Angels surrounding God's Throne will sing God's praise. Unbelievers have rejected clears signs and warnings. No amount of worldly wealth will be enough to ransom their souls. There is no crookedness in the Qur'an. The Qur'an, revealed in Arabic, repeats itself for better instruction yet it is always consistent with itself.

The 85 verses of Surah 40, "Forgiver", begin with cryptic letters followed by an affirmation of the status of the Qur'an as revealed by the one who "forgives". Revelation and rejection, good and evil, truth and falsehood are contrasted (Ali, 1203). We are assured that when we turn to God, revelation, the good and truth aid us in defeating ignorance, unbelief and evil. We again meet Moses before Pharaoh (21–7) and a lone Egyptian believer, who pleaded Moses' case when Pharaoh resolved to kill him. It was, of course, Pharaoh who met his death (37). The people of Noah, 'Ad and Thamud appear at verse 31. A vivid description of hell can be seen at 69–76 but God's promise to the repentant is true. The conceited think they have no need for God, rejecting God's Books. God allocates each of our life-spans, from conception to old age (67). Surahs 40 to 46 are related; they begin with the same cryptic letters. The 54 verses of Surah 41 declare that the Qur'an is "good news" in clear, easy to understand Arabic, expounding the truth (from which the *surah* is named). Only an Arabic scripture can communicate to Arab people. Muhammad is a man like other men but received inspiration from God. Charity and regular prayer will be rewarded but sinners punished. Stories of people rejecting their prophets and of their fate follow. Verse 34 says that we must not repel evil with evil but with what is better and should find ways of turning enemies into friends. Here, Muslims are invited to enter friendly relations with all peoples of the world.

"Shura" (Surah 42) is named after verse 38, which will become an important concept. The believers, soon to become Muslims, are described as "those who govern their affairs by mutual consultation". The content of the chapter assures the believers that good will defeat evil by the help and guidance found in this very Book, that is, the Qur'an. The reference to recompense for injury as equal to the injury given begins to shift us, as does the concept of *Shura*, into the next phase of Muhammad's life and of Muslim history. It is after the migration to Yathrib (renamed Medina) that a social-political-juridical system is established, guided by the Qur'an. The earlier, more general ethical demands of giving to the needy are now fleshed out with specific penalties for crimes, and rules relating to marriage, inheritance and divorce. As elsewhere, the prescribed penalty for injury is immediately followed by encouragement to forgive, to seek reconciliation. Reference to the Arabic nature of the Qur'an (verse 7) is linked with the special status of Mecca as the "mother of cities" (see also 6: 92), which, Ali comments, "is the centre of Islam" while all around her "is the whole world". Here we have the relationship between the particularity of the Qur'an's Arabic and the universality of its message; from Mecca, Islam spreads throughout the world, but its ideals remain firmly rooted in the ethos and ideals of what become a Muslim Mecca. Verse 52 describes the Qur'an as a Light (God, too, is Light) that guides us along the straight path, however dark our journey seems. The concept of consultation suggests that all Muslims have an equal right to participate in governance, as opposed to the argument that those whom God has exalted in rank (17: 21; 6: 165) ought to govern. God, who hears and sees everything, is above all comparison. I discuss this verse, 11, in my Conclusion.

Surah 43, "The Gold Adornment", also affirms the Arabic nature of the Qur'an and the clarity of its message. Verse 4 refers to the "Mother of the Book" (*um-al-kitab*). This resides, as it were, in Allah's own presence (Ali, 43). From this, the Preserved or Heavenly Tablet (*Luh-al-Mahfuz*) was penned by the angels, as the gradual process of the descent of God's word began. Or, the Mother of the Book is identical with the Preserved from which Gabriel brought the revelations in stages down to Muhammad, until during Muhammad's final year he rehearsed the whole of the Qur'an with him, who thus received his Revelation twice, as did Moses. Some sources reverse this, so that Muhammad first received it fully on the Night of Power, then "in fragments during the course of his twenty-three year prophetic career" (Fischer and Abedi, 103; Denffer, 24). As God's word, however, the Qur'an is "eternal", not created even though it also exists as a permanent, written record. The process through which God's thought or spoken word first becomes a heavenly tablet, then a recitation communicated to the prophet, suggests that God communicates through intermediaries because we are too frail to encounter God in the fullness of God's being. *Daraja* occurs again at verse 32. Here, the higher rank appears negative; some people amass wealth but God's mercy has far greater value. Surah 42: 51 says, "Man only speaks with Allah through a veil (*hijab*) or through an Angel, to communicate what God wishes." This verse also suggests that God has sent down sufficient to allow us to enter a relationship with God but has not revealed the totality of who God is. The occurrences of *hijab* discussed so far, interestingly, have nothing to do with how Muslim women or men are expected to dress. People who place value in gold ornaments (verse 43) will one day realize that what glitters has no ultimate value; there is no relationship between material wealth and spiritual health. Evil people often think they are walking along the right path.

Analysis

The remaining Meccan *surahs* will be paraphrased in Chapter 3, which follows the Prophet and his companions as they migrate to Medina, then begins to explore how Islam took shape and developed in that new setting. As we move towards the end of the Meccan period, the chapters have grown longer and their content has started to delineate distinctive features of Islamic practice, even law with at least dietary rules in place. We see how, as the same prophets and their stories are revisited, additions are also made to the storyline. Audiences may be different, or repetition reminds listeners of the basic narrative to which information relevant to the particular context is added (see 39: 23). It does appear that some familiarity with the stories of the prophets was assumed of at least some of Muhammad's listeners.

What has been added to our understanding of the Qur'an on God, humanity and itself? God's Unity is central although the notion of God's Beautiful Names challenges any simplistic ideas of God; each Name represents a quality, or attribute, opening us up to complexity and profundity in thinking about God. God's concern for the animal world, too, has become more explicit; the she-camel, animals safely in the ark, God enabling Solomon to communicate with the birds. On humanity, we learn that our role is one of a steward or trustee of the earth, that we have a responsibility to share resources with animals as well. Creatures are not to be needlessly harmed. On the Qur'an, we have learnt more about the process of revelation, about the stages of descent. We have learned that the Qur'an is able to reach into the heart of an *Umar*, transforming him from an opponent to a champion of God's word. The Qur'an, too, is distinguishing itself from earlier scripture, claiming immunity from corruption and error. So far, no passage has presented any serious exegetical issues.

3 The Community Takes Shape

With dietary rules, the beginning of a legal system in place and the command to order its affairs by consultation, the community that became the Muslim *ummah* was already taking shape towards the end of the Meccan period. The distinction between Muhammad at Mecca as spiritual leader supposedly without political authority and Muhammad at Medina as transformed overnight into a spiritual and political leader is open to challenge. At Mecca he did not govern a state, but as far as his companions were concerned he was leader of their movement, which all along was developing into more than a set of religious beliefs and practices. Islam was always meant to be a total way of life, which is the logic of *tawhid*. As we cover the remaining Meccan chapter to bring us up to the *hijrah*, the migration from Mecca to Yathrib (which soon become known as Madinah-al-nabi, city of the prophet), I argue that it is artificial to supply a clean break between the Meccan and Medinan periods. Debate about which was the final chapter revealed at Mecca and the first at Medina, and chapters sitting astride this seemingly radical division, suggest that no real divide exists between the two periods. Of course, the *hijrah* does mark the birth of the Muslim community and the start of the Islamic calendar, so it must be seen as a highly significant event. Nonetheless, as an event, *hijrah* is best understood rooted in the contexts that preceded and followed it. Developments already in hand in the later Meccan *surahs* continue in the new setting. The real challenge at this juncture is to do justice to these lengthier chapters just as more contextual information becomes available. Paraphrasing in the detail of earlier chapters is problematic. On the other hand, we have now met with most if not all of the prophets and are familiar with how the Qur'an handles aspects of their narratives, so we can concentrate on new material and on what is especially significant in each passage. Following Zarkashi, we pick up from Surah 43 with 44 to 46 in numerical sequence.

Surah 44, "The Smoke". Beginning with cryptic letters, this chapter has 59 verses. The title is from verse 10, where according to Ali "smoke" might refer to a famine in Mecca around about 618 or 619. Again, the Qur'an is presented as a book with clear guidance, sent down on a "blessed night" from God's own presence as a mercy for humanity. There is no God but God and that God is the Lord and Cherisher of all the worlds. The famine may be represented here as divine punishment on the Quraysh for rejecting the Qur'an. They have a messenger with a clear message (verse 58) yet, accusing the messenger of being tutored by someone else, other than God, they call him possessed. Warnings follow a by now familiar pattern; earlier peoples also had their messengers but refused to listen. Again we see Pharaoh at the parted sea (24) and the Children of Israel safely delivered. Verse 43 introduces a new metaphor, the tree of Zaqqum. This tree will feed the sinful. However, this food resembles molten brass and boiling water.

Surah 45, "The Kneeling Down". This chapter of 37 verses is again shorter and also begins with cryptic letters. God, exalted in power and full of Wisdom, is author of the Book. Creation witnesses not only God's power and majesty but also God's mercy; day follows night, rivers flow into the sea, animals are scattered across the globe, indicative of the goodness and kindness of the God of all that is. Yet women and men are ungrateful, refusing to accept the Truth. Verse 12 picks up on the reference at 17: 66 to the ships that sail the sea as a mercy from God, allowing us to seek God's bounty. The ungrateful will be made to kneel on Judgement Day. In subsequent verses, we encounter criticism of the Children of Israel, building on the charge of "concealment" at 6: 91. Despite God's clear signs to them, the Jews "fell into schism" through envy. Finally, God again declares that none of us need fear that the same fate waits for the wicked and for the good.

Surah 46, "Winding Sand-Tracts". With 35 verses, this is a little shorter than both the above. All these related chapters, 40–46, are said to have been revealed in quick succession. They also all begin with an affirmation about the clarity and authority of the Book. Verse 12 identifies the Book as an "Arabic" revelation, to discipline the unjust. Verse 15 stipulates that kindness to parents is a religious duty, especially to our mothers, who carry us and wean us. The prophet Hud appears in verse 21. The sand-tracts were irrigated fields, the pride of the 'Ad. Refusing to acknowledge God but needing rain, the people rejoiced when they saw an approaching cloud. However, the cloud brought a storm that swept their houses away. Again, this chapter specifically addresses the Quraysh for failing to turn towards God.

Following Zarkashi, Surah 51 is next in sequence. Called "The Winds that Scatter" (mentioned in verse 1), these 60 verses, beginning with a divine oath, have a hymn-like quality. The righteous are contrasted with the wicked as on the one hand those who find joy in what God permits and on the other those who thrive on deceit. The story of Abraham feeding his angelic guests (Genesis 19: 1–3; see 11: 69) is at verses 24–37. Only one just household had been found in the condemned city (Lot's). The examples of Moses, 'Ad and Thamud follow. Muhammad is not mad or possessed but warns with clear signs.

Surah 88, "The Overwhelming Event". Ali also locates this as an earlier passage, which is suggested by its brevity (26 verses) and staccato style. The event is Judgement Day, when the wicked will drink boiling water and the righteous will recline on cushions, sipping from flowing goblets. Surah 18 was next in sequence but we shifted this as appropriate background to Muhammad's debates in Mecca leading up to the so-called "compromise", Surah 53.

Surah 16 is called "The Bees", this name deriving from verse 68. God's mercy in creation is a major motif. Man, created from "sperm", has many blessings; cattle to provide milk, to carry heavy loads, to give pleasure when led to pasture. God has given us horses, mules and donkeys to ride. God taught bees how to build their hives. The word at verse 16 is *wahy* (revelation); thus even bees receive direct instruction from God. Muhammad was renowned for his love of horses, of she-camels and of cats. God causes the sun to shine and the rain to fall. All this is for our pleasure and comfort. God has even created the world as a colourful place, so that we can appreciate its beauty. God set the stars in the night-sky to guide us when we travel. He laid down the rivers in their valleys to feed and water us. God raises a witness from every people. Muhammad's task is to persuade people by beautiful preaching and courteous, gracious dialogue (125). Muslims regard this verse as offering guidance on how conflict should be resolved, through gentle persuasion, dialogue and diplomacy. Some argue, though, that later passages permitting use of arms abrogate this verse. Verse 106 of this chapter is one of two that became the basis of the theory of abrogation, that some later verses cancel some earlier verses.

Surah 71, "Noah". With 28 verses, this could also be dated earlier but is located here in our sequence. Brevity indicates an early date but the narrative suggests later. This is the third *surah*, so far, named after a biblical prophet. Another follows. As with the beautifully narrated story of Joseph, which remained on theme, this *surah* stays with Noah from start to finish. Noah's warning to his people, referenced several times (for example at 26: 105), is fleshed out here in more detail. Verse 15 describes Allah as creating seven heavens. There is an interesting allusion at verse 17 to our "growing gradually" and "returning to the earth" which Ali explains as a promise of resurrection. Plants grow, die then return to the earth from which new life is nourished (1535).

Surah 14, "Abraham". Abraham, whom Muhammad met on his Ascent, serves as a model for Muhammad. This chapter starts with cryptic letters. With 52 verses, it is shorter than Noah. Unlike Joseph and Noah but like Mary this *surah* does not only narrate the story of the biblical character after whom it was named. Moses, Noah, the prophets of the 'Ad and the Thamud are alluded to. All their missions were denied by their people. Abraham, says verse 35, was commanded by God to "make this city one of peace and security" and to cleanse it of idolatry. "This City" is taken to be Mecca. Abraham established regular prayers and was gifted with Ishmael and Isaac in old age. Surah 4: 125 calls Abraham *khalil Allah* (God's friend), a high honour since only Abraham is specifically identified in this way.

Surah 21, "The Prophets". Following two chapters named after individual prophets, we now paraphrase one named after all God's messengers. This chapter has 112 verses. Ali identifies it as middle-Meccan (794). Our reckoning draws ever closer, yet we turn away. God has sent prophet after prophet with clear messages, but people reject them. Whole populations have perished because they rejected their prophets. Verse 18 has a vivid phrase – God hurls truth at falsehood, which knocks out its brains. Every messenger teaches that there is No God but God. Tradition says that every messenger proclaims the *Shahadah*, "There is No God but God" followed by their name as God's messenger, beginning with Adam. Moses' scripture, like the Qur'an, was both a Criterion between right and wrong and a Light to lighten the darkness, and the souls of women and men. Abraham at verse 58 broke the idols except for the largest, then challenged the people to ask that idol who had destroyed the others. Noah, David, Solomon, Idris, Job and other messengers such as Dhu al Kifl (perhaps Ezekiel) and Dhu al Nun (a title for Jonah) feature in this chapter, as does Mary. Verse 91 says that God breathed God's spirit into her, making her a sign for all people. Verse 92 uses the special word *ummah*, which becomes the name of the Muslim community. Here, the reference appears to be to the brotherhood of all the prophets, who have equal status; but people create division by claiming superiority for their own apostle. Verse 106 again declares that the message of the Qur'an is for the whole world, for all who choose to worship Allah.

Surah 23, "The Believers" (*al-mu'minum*), the term that until the *hijrah* describes those who follow Muhammad. This chapter has 118 verses. Ethical conduct and piety are the marks of those who believe. They pray, give to charity, abstain from illicit sex and keep their word. Verses 12 to 15 describe our existence from conception to death. As have earlier *surahs*, this one celebrates God's bounty to us through creation; cows give us milk and many other benefits too, such as meat. God has sent us a long line of prophets, including Noah and Moses. All were accused of falsehood. Verse 50 describes both Mary and her son as a "sign". Verse 50 also says that she was given respite on "high ground" (see 19: 22–6), which could be the stable besides the Bethlehem inn where there was no room. Verse 52 refers to the unity of the prophets, who form a single brotherhood. It is people who divide religion into competing sects. Verse 62 says that God never burdens us with a load greater than we can bear. Verse 78 ascribes to God our faculties of hearing, sight and understanding, yet we fail to use our reason and intellect to realize the Truth of God's word. Verse 91 condemns *shirk*. Verse 97 invites us to take refuge in God from the Evil One, similar to the formula used during the annual pilgrimage.

Surah 32, "The Prostration". This chapter of 30 verses begins with cryptic letters. Verse 1 affirms that there is no doubt in the Qur'an. The earlier reference to the possible corruption of previous scriptures suggests that there is doubt in these, at least in their present form. Muhammad has not fabricated the Book. He is the prophet of a people to whom no previous messenger has been sent. Many other people have had messengers. They have rejected them. The Children of Israel had many leaders to give them guidance but create division by arguing and dissenting among themselves. God's largesse through creation sends rain to water crops "providing food for cattle" and for ourselves. Therefore, we should fall down in prayer and prostrate ourselves (verse 15) in adoration and praise of God.

Surah 52, "The Mount". This chapter has 49 verses. The Mount is Mount Hira, where Muhammad first received revelation, which is described as an unfolded scroll, again indicative of the self-awareness in the Qur'an of its recorded permanency. As do many of the rhythmic *surahs*, this one works up to a crescendo; in a scroll, by the raised canopy, by the ocean, none can prevent the day from dawning when the earth itself will break apart. The righteous will enter the Garden and find bliss; the wicked hell-fire. Verse 20 brings us companions with "lustrous eyes", verse 24 handsome youths who will serve us. There will be neither frivolity nor sickness. Verse 32 introduces the concept of the Qur'an's inimitability; Muhammad's mockers, who accuse him of producing poetry or of fabricating his messages, are challenged to "produce a recital like the Qur'an". Muslims believe that no literature in Arabic is as eloquently expressive and as exquisite as the Qur'an. Those who wanted Muhammad to perform a miracle to prove his status as God's messenger are advised that the Qur'an is a miracle of language. Those who scoff might try climbing a ladder to heaven, to see if they can acquire God's secrets for themselves, since they reject God's message.

Surah 67, "The Dominion". The name is derived from the first of 30 verses, which proclaims God as having dominion over all that is. God created the seven heavens. In the lowest heavens God has placed lamps to drive evil away. Whenever people face Judgement, they will be asked if a prophet warned them to repent and turn to God. They will say, "Yes, but we rejected him." Then, they will wish that they had used their intellect. That day, they will confess their sins, but their deeds have already determined their fate. Verse 15 says that God has made the earth "manageable" for us, so we are to travel across it and enjoy all its bounty. On that Day, however, the earth itself will be swallowed up. Verse 19 advises us to look at the flight of birds as a sign of how God has adapted each creature to their environment. Muhammad may have been challenged to reveal when Judgement Day will dawn, but no one except Allah knows this. His job is to warn.

Surah 69, "The Sure Reality". The name is from verse 1. The sure reality is that truth will prevail. The people of 'Ad, the Thamud, Noah's people and Pharaoh were all warned, failed to listen and were punished. When the final trumpet sounds, mountains will turn to powder, the sky will be torn across and each of our records will be read. Either we will eat and drink in heaven (of the Right Hand) or we will burn in hell (of the Left). Muhammad is not a *kahini*, or a poet, but God's most honourable messenger, whose revelations are a source of joy for believers, of sorrow for unbelievers.

Surah 70, "The Ways of Ascent". The title is from verse 3. Can we climb up to heaven? Angels can and so can we when spiritually pure. Purity requires prayer, charity, chastity, honesty and sustaining peace in the community. We should seek out the needy, not wait for people to petition us. The needy have a right to share our good fortune, which many Quraysh resented. Verse 4 is one of several indicating that divine time is different from our time; a day for God could be as long as 50,000 years. Muslims, seeing this as an indicative number, apply this to creation over six days (see 7: 54) to suggest harmony between Qur'an and science.

Surah 78, "The Great News". The great news is the promise of paradise for the righteous. God's mercy to us through creation is a major motif; God created us in pairs (so sex is a gift from God), he gave us the ability to sleep for rest, gave us the day to work for our sustenance. In verse 13, "light of splendour" might be a reference to Muhammad (Ali, 1586). When the final trumpet sounds, the heavens will open like doors. The wicked enter hell where nothing cool will quench their thirst; the righteous heaven where cups will be full to the brim. It is deeds that determine our fate. God may allow some to plead mercy for sinners on that day. Justice, though, will never be compromised. Against the popular view that Muslims are fatalistic, the Qur'an insists that we choose which path we tread.

Surah 79, "Those Who Tear Out". The title, from verse one of 46 verses, refers to the angels who will tear out the souls of the wicked on Judgement Day. Just as Moses warned Pharoah, who did not listen, so Muhammad is a warner for those who choose to hear.

Surah 82, "The Cleaving Asunder". This image of the earth being torn apart has emerged as a recurring and powerful motif. Kind and honourable angels record our deeds. God has gifted us with a bias towards justice, with intelligence and reason. We can live lives that please God. While we live, we can help our sisters and brothers but once that Day dawns, we stand alone. The opening five verses are rhythmic, building up from "when the sky is cleft asunder" through "when the graves are turned upside-down" to each of us knowing what we did and what we failed to do (Ali, 1612).

Surah 84, "The Rending Asunder". The imagery used in these 25 verses is similar to that of Surah 82. Again, the opening verses build up to a climax. Here, despite hardship and suffering and effort, if we do what is right we will meet our Lord. This world is real but it will end. The next world is where true values will last for ever. The unregenerate fail to recognize the truth of the Qur'an, fail to fall prostrate before its eloquence. The opening phrase, "when the sky is rent asunder" is, effectively, also the ending (Ali, 1622).

Surah 30, "The Romans". Beginning with cryptic letters, this is a chapter of 60 verses. The name is from verse 2, which declares that the Roman Empire has been defeated. This is a historical reference to the Byzantine Empire under Heraclius, to whom Muhammad later wrote. The empire was losing territory to Persia. The ebb and flow of empires, suggests Ali in his summary, "are outward events: the deeper meaning is in the working of Allah's universe – how good and evil reach their final end" (1006). Here, God is represented as Lord of history. Even when we can not fully understand how events advance the cause of providence, the triumph of the good, God is working God's purposes out. In the end, those who do evil will reap an evil reward. No intercessor, or partner of God, will plead their case. Believers and those who did what was right enter heaven. Verse 21 describes marriage as a blessing; spouses are gifts of "tranquility" to each other. Verse 22 tells us that our different languages and colours are signs from God "for those who know". Despite our differences, we are a single human race, all people are equally precious to God. Evil people follow their own lust and desire. God demands exclusive worship; we can not worship Allah while still giving part-worship to other gods. As at 6: 11 we are invited to travel the world to see what happened to previous, unrepentant people. Instead, we should embrace the right Religion and prepare for the Hour of Reckoning. Verse 46 again refers to ships that sail across the seas as a mercy, enabling us to benefit from God's bounty, for which gratitude is due.

Surah 83, "The Dealers in Fraud". Several earlier *surahs* refer to believers as those who give measure for measure, who keep their word and trade fairly. This chapter of 36 verses condemns "fraud" in all matters, mundane as well as spiritual (Ali, 1615). As we near the end of Meccan verses and track the establishment of the "state" over which Muhammad would soon preside, the Qur'an brings every aspect of life under its remit. The honest businessman is worshipping God when he trades just as he when he prays. *Ibadat*, worship, is derived from *abd*, or "servant" (sometimes rendered "slave"). Our deeds are recorded on Registers; only the honest will see God's light. Sitting on raised couches, they will see everything that can be seen, including, some commentators say, God's Face as Muhammad apparently did on his night journey (see Parsons, 152–4). The wicked confuse, or exchange, falsehood for truth.

Surah 29, "The Spider". Following our sequence, this is the final Meccan *surah*. Pickthall thinks that the latter portion may have been revealed at Medina. If so, this is an appropriate bridge to link us to the story of the migration and to the earliest post-migration *surahs* to which we turn in this chapter. This *surah* "gives comfort to Muslims in time of persecution" (Pickthall, 413). It begins with cryptic letters. In the following 69 verses, there is much material with which we are by now familiar. Verse 7 says that when we "work righteous deeds" God will "blot out all the evil that is in us", indicating that salvation is not achieved *only by work* but *also requires God's mercy*, which works within us. Surah 4: 99 says that God repeatedly blots out our sins. God knows who we really are, whether our claim to believe is genuine, or hypocritical. Noah, Abraham, Lot, the Midianites, Moses, the people of 'Ad and the Thamud, all feature in these verses. For all their worldly power, those who oppose God build nothing more substantial than spiders' webs, a beautiful metaphor (verse 41). Verse 43 says that only those with knowledge can understand the parables God communicates. Some interpret this to mean that a few can claim special knowledge. Ali suggests that everyone who trusts in God attains such knowledge, by God's grace (997).

Verses 45 to 51 represent important new content in our journey through the 114 chapters of the Qur'an. Verse 46 introduces us for the first time to the term, "people of the Book" (*ahlu-al-kitab*). This term will become more familiar as we move into the post-migration period. It refers to Jews, Christians and to other monotheists who possess scriptures given to previous prophets. Verse 46 instructs Muhammad, and therefore all Muslims, not to dispute with the Scriptuaries except if they are wrongdoers but to employ "better means", saying, "we believe in your revelation and in ours, since your God and our God is One". Here, as it does elsewhere, the Qur'an affirms that Jews, Christians and Muslims worship the same God. Followers of these faiths should not engage in polemic or diatribe but in dialogue, which is a better means. By establishing common ground, we realize that we all bow to the same God. More will be said about the status of people of the book and about Islam's relationship with other religions as we encounter other verses on this topic. With 16: 125, this verse is understood as giving guidance on how conflict is to be handled; it calls for non-violent diplomacy and dialogue. Al-Ghazali, though, devotes several paragraphs here to castigate the West for aggressive behaviour against Muslims, for vilifying Islam and for directing "derision and abuse … at the Qur'an". There are, he says, "powers in the world today that do not wish Islam to prosper or spread" (Ghazali and Shamis, vol. 2, pp. 202–3).

The *Hijrah*

This brings us to the critical event known as the *hijrah*, or migration which took place in September 622. According to Zarkash, the next cluster of *surahs* are 2, 8, 3, 33, 60, 4 and 22. Of these, 2 is considered very early Medinan; 3 and 4 are both identified with the Battle of Uhud, which took place in March 625, so can be dated with some precision; 22 is thought to sit astride the Mecca–Medina divide, so-called. Verse 40 is traditionally taken to be the first passage permitting self-defence, so must predate similar verses in Surah 2. Surah 8 on the "Spoils of War" is taken to date from soon after the Battle of Badr (March

624) while 33 is linked with the Battle of the Trench, which occurred in March 627. Surah 60, thought to be after the Treaty of Hudaybiyah had been broken, is discussed in Chapter 4. We will therefore treat the verses in the following sequence, 22, 2, 8, 3, 4 and 33. This chapter deals with 22 to 4. The next chapter picks up from 33.

According to Pickthall, in Surah 22, verses 11–13, 25–30, 39–41 and 58–60 were revealed at Medina (Pickthall, 337). Ibn Ishaq, however, states that verse 40 was revealed to Muhammad before the migration as actually enabling the *hijrah* to take place; "The prophet had not been given permission to fight or allowed to take blood before the second 'Aqaba" but had "simply been ordered to call men to God and to endure insult and forgive the ignorant". Then 22: 39–40 gave him "permission to fight" (*yuqataloona*, from *qital*) but only "because their sole offence ... has been that they worship God" yet are "unjustly treated". After this, with the converts in Medina ready to give him refuge, Muhammad "commanded his companions ... to emigrate to Medina and link with his brethren, the Ansars" (Guillaume, 212–13). The Ansars, or helpers, were those who had taken the pledges of Aqaba. Muhammad with Abu Bakr and Ali supervised the migration, remaining in Mecca until those who could do so had left. Some were restrained from leaving by the Quraysh while a few apostatized (Guillaume, 221). The departure of the believers, though despised, had financial implications, since "many houses would now be tenantless or almost empty" (Lings, 116). In response, Abu Jahl organized a team of volunteers from each clan who set out to eliminate Muhammad. Warned by Gabriel, who told him that it was now time for him to leave the city, Muhammad made plans to do so in Abu Bakr's company, asking Ali to stay behind a few days longer to deal with remaining business. This included returning property that people had entrusted to Muhammad's safe-keeping. Despite everything, his reputation for honesty meant that even unbelievers "would trust him with their property as they would trust no one else" (Lings, 117).

Gabriel also warned Muhammad not to sleep that night in his usual place. Muhammad asked Ali to wear his cloak, in which "no harm would befall him". He then recited from Surah 36, including the verse, "we have clouded their vision so that they cannot see" (9), which allowed Muhammad to slip away unseen. When the assassins realized that Muhammad had escaped, that the person they thought was him was Ali, they hurried off to sound the alarm. Ibn Ishaq says that later Surah 8: 30 was "sent down" about this day, "Remember that when the unbelievers plotted against you, to imprison you or to kill you,

Allah countered their plot, for Allah is the best of plotters." Knowing that his enemies were looking for him, Muhammad and Abu Bakr left through "a window in the back of the latter's house" (Guillaune, 224), heading for a cave, an hour's walk away. The two "stayed in the cave for three days" while their enemies searched high and low (Guillaume, 224). Later, 9: 40 referred to this incident, saying that "when the unbelievers compelled" Muhammad to "leave, there was but one companion with him in the Cave". Muhammad then said to his companion, "Do not fear, for Allah is with us and sends down His peace. Allah thus supported him with unseen strength, humbling the word of his enemies with God's own, exalted Word." It was at that very moment that several men passed by the cave, listened, agreed that there was no need to enter because no one was there, and left. Muhammad is cited to have said, "What thinkest thou", asked the prophet, "of two when God is their third?" (Lings, 119) From the cave, a 12-day journey followed. Before completing the final leg to Medina, Muhammad stayed at a supporter's home in Quba, where Ali joined him. Abu Bakr stayed at Sunh, "a little nearer to Madina" (Lings, 121).

While Muhammad was in Quba, a man called Rozeba became a believer. Born in Persia and originally Zoroastrian, Rozeba had converted to Christianity in his teens. One day, a bishop had predicted that he would meet a prophet, marked with the "seal" on his back. This prophet would be migrating to Medina and never ate any food given as alms. On his journey to find this prophet, Rozeba was sold into slavery by merchants whom he had paid to take him to Medina. Hearing about Muhammad, he slipped away from his master's house, went to where Muhammad was staying and offered food, "specifying that he gave it as alms". Muhammad fed this to his companions but ate none himself. There and then, Rozeba became a believer. He was renamed Salman (protector) by Muhammad; he hoped one day also to see the seal of prophecy (Lings, 122). Later, Salman al-Farsi was able to buy his freedom with help from Muslim friends. Shortly after, he played a significant role at the Battle of the Trench. He went on to translate segments of the Qur'an into Persian and to serve, although only for a few weeks before his death at aged 88, as governor of Madaen in Iraq during Abu Bakr's caliphate. Muhammad spent three days in Quba, where he began to build the very first *masjid* (mosque) (Lings, 123). There, Muhammad led Friday congregational prayer and preached the first *khutbah* in Isalam.

Muhammad entered Medina on 22 September 622. Looking for a place to stay, he was attracted by a walled courtyard containing a few "date palms and a ruined building", so enquired if he could purchase this property (Lings, 124).

The owners, two orphans, wanted to give it to him but he insisted on paying them, so a price was agreed. Immediately, he ordered that a mosque and living quarters be built, staying with a distant relative and Ansari leader, Abu Ayyub until the mosque and attached accommodation was complete. This was a simple structure, about "36 yards by 30". There "was a covered area, with a roof of palm branches, thatched and daubed, resting on palm trunks". When not used for prayer, the courtyard functioned as public space. Rooms backing onto the East wall accommodated Muhammad and his family (Reeves, 31–2). A stone marked the *qiblah* (direction of prayer). There was no dome or minaret, which developed later as architectural features. A *mimbar*, to the right of the *qiblah*, with three steps, was constructed for Muhammad to sit on when giving the Friday *Khutbah* (address, sermon). As soon as the mosque was complete, Muhammad initiated the routine of five daily prayers preceded by ritual ablution (*wudu*), the compulsory Friday congregational (*jumma*) prayers for men including the *Khutbah*, the *zakat* (donation to the poor) and the annual fast. It was not until the ninth year of the *hijrah* that pilgrimage was added as the fifth pillar. The term "five pillars" is found in the *hadith*, for example, at Bukhari 2: 7. Al-Ghazali points out that all five pillars, the *shahada* (21), prayer (238), charity (254), fasting (183) and pilgrimage (196), are mentioned in Surah 2, which we summarize shortly (Ghazali and Shamis, vol. 1, p. 18). He takes 2 to be the first Medinan *surah* (19). Rules concerning all five pillars are found in the next cluster of *surahs*. Ibn Ishaq says that with the five pillars in place, Islam "took up its abode with" the community (Guillaume, 235). The call to prayer (*adhzan*) was also introduced. Muhammad thought about using a trumpet or bells, then a clapper. He was having this made when a close companion had a dream, in which the words of the call to prayer were spoken to him. Hearing the words, Muhammad declared that they were from God and immediately commissioned Bilal, an African Muslim, to act as the first *muezzin* or *muedhin* (from *aana*, to call). Bilal walked the streets reciting the call, then recited it more quietly in the prayer hall. The five prayer times, dawn, a little after noon, afternoon, after sunset, before dusk, can be found in this sequence at Bukhari 10: 500.

Permission to "Fight"

Surah 22, entitled "Pilgrimage", has 78 verses. Despite the coming terror of Judgement people still dispute with God, and some even choose Satan's counsel. Verse 5 says that God causes our birth, oversees our upbringing and ends our lives as God wills. God gives life. God is all powerful and will raise us all up. Allah is always just. Some serve God until life becomes difficult, when they backslide and call on false gods to help them. God admits believers, who act righteously, into the Garden. On Judgement Day, God will adjudicate between the disputes of the believers, Jews, Sabaeans (possibly Gnostic), Christians, Magians (Zoroastrians) and Polytheists. The sun, hills, trees and animals all worship God. Rivers flow beneath the promised Gardens. Those who reside there will wear jewellery and fine silk. Verse 25 refers to Mecca, the Sacred Mosque which God has opened for all people. Verse 26 introduced the pilgrimage, which gives this *surah* its name. Abraham proclaimed the pilgrimage and sanctified the Ka'bah. The mention at verse 28 of cattle for sacrifice is interpreted as referring to Eid-al-Adha, the 10th day of the month of *hajj* (Ali, 828). Verse 29 on pilgrims fulfilling their vows indicates the importance of the inner, spiritual *hajj*, without which the physical pilgrimage is worthless. This is sometimes represented as the need for *iman*, faith, and *Islam* as external obedience to be harmonized. Every nation has its own prescribed rites (37, repeated at 67). God is interested in the hearts of those who sacrifice, not in offerings of flesh and blood. Verse 39 shifts from pilgrimage to defence when oppressed, permitting this for the first time. When you are unjustly expelled from your homes merely because you believe in God, when places of worship are destroyed, permission is given to fight (*qital*). Here, places of worship include churches and synagogues as well as mosques. Ibn Kathir, citing Ibn Abbas, calls this the first verse of *jihad*, which was revealed now because it "would have been disastrous" for him to have fought while at Mecca (6: 584). Having been "expelled from their homes unjustly" permission was now given "at an appropriate time". Later, the tradition discussed whether migration was voluntary or whether the Muslims were compelled to flee; according to Ibn Kathir, they were "driven out of Makkah".

The Medinan Covenant

With permission to defend against oppression, Muhammad and the *muhajirun* had a way to gain compensation for their lost property, which they heard was being sold off by the Quraysh. Muhammad was now head of his community of Muslims, *ansaris* and *muhajirun*, who recognized him as political as well as spiritual leader. Before the end of the first year AH, he consolidated this position by entering a covenant with the Jewish tribes of Medina, often referred to as the Constitution of Medina, which was a written document (Guillaume, 231–3). The Muslims and those who labour with them form a single *ummah* (community). All disputes are to be adjudicated by Muhammad. No one is to make war without Muhammad's permission. The peace of the community is indivisible. Conditions must be "fair and equitable". The Jews are to contribute financially to their defence. No Quraysh, sinner or the unjust are to be protected. "Loyalty", says the covenant, "is a protection from treachery." Two specific contexts are behind the revelation of Surah 2, "The Cow". First, although the Jewish tribes had entered into the covenant, this did not mean that their Rabbis were happy with Muhammad's religious claims and some expressed hostility towards him. In this, they were joined by the hypocrites, men who had publicly embraced Islam but who secretly "clung to their heathen religion" (Guillaume, 239). Ibn Ishaq says that the first 100 verses of Surah 2 "came down in reference to these Jewish Rabbis and the hypocrites" (Guillaume, 247). There were also Jews who embraced Islam, such as Kab ak-Ahbar, who narrated *hadith*, and the respected Rabbi, Husayn Ibn Sallam, renowned for his loyalty to and love for Muhammad as well as for the beauty of his Qur'anic recitation.

Many encounters were taking place between Muhammad and Jews as well as Christians at this time, reflected in the content of the *surah* which deals in detail with Muslim–non-Muslim relations. Second, having received permission to take action to compensate for their losses, about a year after arriving in Medina, a series of raids began against Quraysh caravans. Ibn Ishaq comments that only emigrants took part in at least the first of these, since it was they who had been driven from their homes (Guillaume, 281). Several verses in Surah 2 reaffirm permission to use war as a response to injustice, while also indicating that war is a distasteful necessity. One specific context relates to a raid led by 'Abdullah Ibn Jahsh, whose men encountered a caravan at Nakhla on the very eve of a Sacred Month. They were reluctant to attack, realizing this would encroach on the amnesty, but also knew that if they missed the opportunity, they would suffer hardship. However, when they took the prisoners and goods to Muhammad, he chastised them for fighting in the Sacred Month. He refused to distribute what had been recovered. Then verse 217 was revealed, confirming the seriousness of breaking the armistice, but also affirming that to be driven from home and prevented from worshipping at the Sacred Mosque was even more serious. Fighting is permitted in these circumstances, providing that aggression is met by an equivalent response.

Victory at Badr

The Battle of Badr took place about six months after the raid at Nakhla, when a force of 1,000 Quraysh set out to defeat the Muslims, who fielded only 314 men, but were themselves defeated. The Quraysh lost 50 including Abu Jahl, the Muslims 8 (Guillaume, 337–8). It was after Badr that Abu Sufyan became leader of the Quraysh. Some verses dealing with war in Surah 2, such as 190-1, are taken to be later, possibly after the Treaty of Hudaybiyya (628) which allowed the Muslims to perform the *hajj*. Verse 191 has been interpreted as permitting almost unlimited aggression, the first verse we encounter so far that has been understood to support the later territorial expansion of the Islamic polity. Verse 191 may not originally have been linked with 190, which, if the above interpretation is correct, it contradicts (see Firestone, 55, 85, 154 n. 68). Firestone suggests that war verses were "joined together in the editing process" (85).

The name of Surah 2 is taken from the story at verses 67–73. As well as addressing hypocrites, Jews and dealing with war, verses also outline the "basic foundations or pillars of Islam" (Ghazali and Shamis, 26), and lay down dietary rules and rules related to marriage and divorce, the first we have encountered. These include verses concerning gender, several of which have attracted controversy. Given the length of the *surahs* we are now discussing, I do not attempt to paraphrase their entire content. Verses 1 to 39 address hypocrites, of which 30 to 39 cover the Adam–Eve story. Verse 2 affirms that there is no doubt in the Qur'an, implying that there is doubt in earlier scriptures as these have been handed down. Hypocrites may try to block out the sound of thunder during a storm but they cannot escape the thunderbolt that is to come. They ridicule Muhammad, yet could not if challenged produce a single *surah* to rival the matchless Qur'an. Those who break their covenant with God will be compounded in their wickedness, since they have hardened their hearts against the truth.

The purpose of this Adam–Eve story is to stress humanity's exalted status, which individuals ought to honour. In this account, when God tells the angels that he is about to place a *Khalif* (deputy) on earth, they object that he will cause havoc, while they serve God and sing God's praise. Replying that God knows what they do not know, he places Adam on earth then tells him the name of all creatures. In Genesis, Adam names the animals. When challenged to name the animals, the angels are unable to do so, so Adam teaches them. The point here is that although humanity does shed blood and create mischief, being gifted with special *ilm* (knowledge), people can also steward the earth properly and obey God as a matter of choice. Lacking free will, angels do what they do because they have no alternative. Again, only the jinn, Iblis refuses to bow before Adam. Adam and Eve are allowed to eat all the fruits in the Garden except one. Tempted by Satan, they eat that fruit and are expelled, or "sent down". Ali takes this to imply that the Garden was non-terrestrial (25 n. 50). He also takes use of the plural at verse 36 to represent Adam as a "type of all mankind" because the Arabic "you" here implies more than two people. God, however, repents or relents towards Adam, and gives him words of inspiration (*kalam*). Eve, known as Hawwa by Muslims, is not named in the Qur'an, which refers to her as Adam's wife. Passages such as 35: 11 and 4: 1 imply that man and woman were simultaneously created from the same sperm, or soul. However, Ibn Kathir, citing Ibn Abbas, chooses to supply here the tradition of God taking one of Adam's ribs to form Eve, which is not found in the Qur'an (Ibn Kathir, vol. 1, p. 197). Humanity is by nature *muslim* but forgets (see Surah 59: 19). God, ever merciful, continually reminds humanity through prophet, Book and nature itself, which is also a type of Book. Shifting to address the Children of Israel, the word "remember" becomes a constant refrain, almost biblical in its relentless insistence that the Jews *remember* what God did for them in the Exodus, itself so critical within Jewish faith. A central motif here is the charge of *tahrif*, that Jews conceal the meaning of their scripture or even fabricate content, writing down what Allah did not reveal. Verses such as 83 and 177, calling for kindness to parents, orphans and the poor, for regular prayer and charity and encouraging the manumission of slaves, also resonate with the biblical demand for moral conduct, that justice should flow down like waters and righteousness like an ever flowing stream (Amos 5: 24). In fact, this is described as the substance of God's covenant with the children of Israel. Abraham's centrality in this *surah* shows that, even as Islam was emerging as a distinct *din* (religion), it continued to regard Abraham as an important patriarchal figure.

Interreligious Relations

Verse 104 shifts us into interreligious dialogue between Jews, Christians and Muslims. In what follows, the Qur'an accuses some people of the Book of wanting to subvert Muslim faith. However, the phrase "quite a number" suggests that this does not apply to everyone. With 16: 101, verse 106 became the basis of the theory of abrogation. Muslims regard one such cancelled verse as 2: 62, which appears to affirm that believers, Jews, Christians and Sabaeans who believe in God, the Judgement and live righteously, have no need to fear. This is repeated at 5: 69. This, some argue, is cancelled by 3: 85, which says that God accepts no *din* (religion) other than Islam. Ibn Kathir, citing Ibn Abbas, takes 3: 85 as an abrogating verse. The Scriptuaries here, he says, were Christians and *Jews before the coming of Muhammad*; once Muhammad came, only those who recognize his apostleship are saved (Ibn Kathir, vol. 1, p. 249). Christians and Jews are castigated for making exclusive claims, saying that only Jews or Christians will enter paradise. Both claim to study the same book but interpret it differently. They will never be satisfied until Muslims follow their form of religion. The story of the heifer shows the people all but refusing to offer God a sacrificial cow by haggling over which cow, finally asking what colour it had to be. Verse 142 makes Mecca the direction of prayer, which had previously been Jerusalem. Although there is no verse on Jerusalem as the *qiblah*, this change created some disquiet. Arguably, the change consolidates Islam as a distinctive religious path, indicated by verse 143 on the *ummah* as "justly balanced". Verse 158 describes aspects of the rite of *hajj*, running between Safa and Marwah. Verse 196 mentions the *umrah*, the pilgrimage that can be performed at other times of the year. Those whose circumstances prevent them performing the *hajj* should fast, feed the poor or pay for an Eid celebration. Fasting for the required number of days during Ramadan is prescribed at verses 184–7. Travellers and the sick can make up when able. Sexual relations are permitted at night.

Gender Equality

Verse 164 repeats one of my favourite Qur'anic affirmations, that ships sailing across the seas are a sign of divine mercy. Verse 173 prohibits consumption of pork and anything over which God's name has not been invoked. Verse 178 adjudicates for murder, calling for equity, that is, the death penalty. However, this is immediately qualified by encouraging forgiveness; relatives of the victim ought to consider accepting compensation instead (see also 4: 92–3). Verse 219 says that the sin of consuming alcohol and of gambling outweighs the benefit (see also 4: 43; 5: 93–4). Next, passages deal with inheritance, presenting us with the first cluster of what might be described as legal material. No longer governed by the customs of Meccan society, the *ummah* now required its own laws. Controversy has centred on verses 223 and 228. Verse 223 describes wives as "fields" for their husbands, which they can enjoy at will. This is said to justify non-consensual sex within marriage, although most of the *hadith* surrounding this verse discuss which sexual positions are permitted. If mutuality seems lacking here, this can be set alongside 30: 21, which says that spouses are a gift to each other. Surah 4: 19 is interpreted to prohibit non-consensual sex, which is rape. Here verse 228 says that women's rights are similar to men's, but that men's rights are a "step" (*darajah*) above theirs. Ali interprets men's rights here more as responsibilities; men in Islam have a duty to support women relatives (92 n. 255). Al-Ghazali fully supports a woman's right to petition for divorce with or without reason, just as a man can pronounce divorce with or without reason (Ghazali and Shamis, vol. 1, p. 31). Surah 4: 128 is taken as providing women the right to petition for divorce. Verses in this segment specify that reconciliation is always the best option. There is to be a four-month period of waiting (*iddah*) to facilitate reconciliation and also to see if the wife is pregnant. Arrangements deal with this situation. An irrevocable divorce means that a woman must first marry someone else then obtain a divorce before she can re-marry her previous husband. There is a one-off alimony payment (241). Women retain the *Mahr* (bridal gift) unless they choose to return any of this by way of an equitable settlement (229).

Turning to commercial matters, Verse 275 condemns usury. Muslims charge a fixed, agreed fee, not adjustable interest. Verse 282, the longest in the entire Qur'an, has also attracted controversy. After stipulating that business transactions should be recorded, this verse says that if dispute arises and the matter goes to adjudication one man or two women may give evidence. This has led to the expression that women are worth half of men. This provision has been defended on the grounds that women were, at the time, unused to giving evidence in court or perhaps to business in general. Liberal Muslims suggest that this provision was temporary, an improvement on pre-Islamic practice that excluded women's evidence, although we can only speculate on pre-Islamic customs. The ethical spirit of such improvements, they say, logically implies complete equality and the provisional nature of the half-a-man rule on evidence.

The shift to war occurs at verse 190, which again permits defence against aggression but Muslims are not to "transgress limits". Many regard this as giving measure for measure without retaliating excessively. Those who argue that the next verse cancels this, understand the "limit" to mean that non-combatants must not be harmed. Verse 191, which has been interpreted to justify almost unlimited aggression, says, "slay unbelievers wherever you find them but do not fight them at the Sacred Mosque unless they attack you first". This may respond to Muslim fear that despite Hudaybiyya, they might be attacked while performing the *hajj*. Yet verse 193 continues, "fight (*waqatiloo*) until there is no more oppression (*fitnah*)". *Fitnah* can also mean sedition. However, the verse suggests the same limited permission for war found in 22: 40, although some Muslims have interpreted this as commanding "anything but moderation", allowing aggression "until Islam becomes the hegemonic power" (Firestone, 85). Many liberal and progressive Muslims could be cited who argue that verse 191 remains conditional; some argue that war is only ever justified as a last resort. Verse 216 says that the Muslims found war distasteful, even when it was a pragmatic necessity. Interestingly, however, Ibn Kathir and Al-Ghazali, both conservatives, are emphatic that the Qur'an does not permit aggression. Ibn Kathir rejects 9: 5 as an abrogating verse, arguing that Muslims are only permitted to fight against aggression (Ibn Kathir, vol. 1, p. 527). Al-Ghazali describes the view that the Qur'an anywhere prescribes "waging war against those who do not commit aggression" as a "gross misunderstanding" (Ghazali and Shamis, vol. 1, p. 162). Muslims have mistakenly used 2: 191 and 9: 5 to justify "conquests which took place in Egypt, Syria and Iraq" so that Muslim armies swept "over the whole of the Persian and a large part of the Byzantine empires" (Ghazali and Shamis, vol. 1, p. 160). Muslims love peace and are committed to diplomacy and peaceful persuasion. No prophet could be a warmonger. Verse 246 also refers to fighting only in response to injustice. Yet it was Al-Ghazali who gave evidence in June 1993 in defence of the killer of the Egyptian columnist and intellectual Farag Foda, arguing that it was permissible to kill an apostate (Kepel 2006, 287). In close proximity to several war-verses are such statements as "make peace whenever your foe invites this" and stop when oppression ceases. Muslims have used 2: 192 to permit armed suppression of sedition that compromises the unity of Islam. Verse 217 is related to the incident at Nakhla. Verse 256 affirms that religious faith is always a matter of choice; no one is to be compelled or forced to embrace Islam, although 9: 5 has been cited to justify the choice between belief and death.

Victory at Badr raised the question of how the "spoils of war" should be distributed. Surah 8, named after verse 1, "they ask you concerning the spoils of war" attributes victory at Badr to God: "you did not slay them, God did" (17). They called on God, who helped them by sending a thousand angels (9).

Verse 42 describes how the Muslims found themselves on higher ground than their attackers. God made the Meccans think that a larger force opposed them, though they still looked at this with contempt. Verse 46 tells the Muslims to obey both God and Muhammad, God's messenger. He is to receive a fifth of war booty as are the needy, widows, orphans and wayfarers. Verse 61 reiterates that peace is preferable, so if the enemy indicates they want peace, reach an agreement with them. Verse 58 relates to the expulsion for treachery of the Banu Qurayzah, who broke the covenant. Verses 67 to 71 deal with the 70 captives taken at Badr, for whom ransom was taken. Here, the Qur'an says that it is wrong to profit from war but that in this instance the Muslims should enjoy what has been lawfully obtained. Several of the prisoners embraced Islam, including the prophet's uncle, Ibn 'Abbas, whose own heirs founded the Abbasid caliphate. This *surah* is also concerned with the unity and faithfulness of the *ummah*, reminding Muslims to trust God. Victory must not fill them with pride, which comes before a fall. This happened in March 225, when the Muslims lost the Battle of Uhud, at which 3,000 Quraysh led by Abu Sufyan confronted about 1,000 Muslims. Initially, the Muslims pushed the enemy back. Then a contingent abandoned their assigned posts, starting to loot the enemy camp. A few hypocrites deserted. Defeat followed. The Muslims lost 65, the Qurayshi 22 (Guillaume, 403). Victory at Badr had been interpreted as a sign of divine blessing. Did defeat mean punishment? Or had God abandoned them? Surah 3 responds to this anxiety.

The Muslim Jesus

The name of Surah 3, "Imran", is taken from verse 33. After the opening cryptic letters, the verse attests that God is "self-subsisting" and sent down the Qur'an to confirm the books of Moses and of Jesus. Jesus' Book is called the *Injil*. Muslims point out that use of the singular implies that Jesus' original book was not the four Gospels, which were written by men, not sent down by God. Indeed, the Gospels resemble *hadith* or *sira* more than scripture. Later verses on *tahrif* shed doubt on whether the *Injil* has survived, such as 71 and 78. The Qur'an is again described as the Criterion between right and wrong. Verse 7, cited in the Introduction, is important for *tafsir*, describing some verses as clear and others as requiring interpretation. While Surah 2 focused on Islam's relationship with Judaism, the focus of Surah 3 is on Christianity. First, we look at the content–context aspects. Verse 19 declares that religion before God is Islam, while verse 110 describes the *ummah* as the best community, an example for all humanity because Muslims prohibit what is wrong and practise what is permitted (see also 104). Verse 122 links with the defeat at Uhud, accusing of cowardice those who began to loot. Verse 152 says that those who went after the booty had their eyes on worldly wealth. They disobeyed Muhammad, who even then was calling them back. Muhammad, however, is instructed to consult (*shura*) before taking decisions (159). Verse 154 says that what took place was a test, so that God could "purge" the Muslims of "all signs of weakness and corruption" (Ghazali and Shamis, vol. 1, p. 49; see verse 141). Had the Muslims stood their ground, God would have aided them as he had at Badr with up to five thousand angels. Muhammad himself was wounded yet even had he died, as earlier prophets have, the Muslims must stand firm. A beautiful verse, 31, says that if we love God, God will love us and forgive us our sins. God does not love wrongdoers. If people love God, they will follow Muhammad (see also 132). It was Satan who caused some to fail. Below, 4: 116 says that God never forgives *shirk*, the sin of associating a partner with God.

Al-Ghazali links the *surahs* dealings with Christianity with a visit to Medina of a Christian delegation. Several verses from this *surah* have played a major role in Muslim–Christian conversation. Verse 35 describes how Mary's mother, the wife of Imran, dedicated the child in her womb to God's service. The birth narratives of John the Baptist and of Jesus follow. Verse 42 speaks of Mary as chosen and purified above all women. Her son would speak from the cradle and in maturity. God would fill him with wisdom. At verse 49, the infant Jesus creates a bird from clay, breathing life into this. By God's leave, Jesus healed the sick, raised the dead and cured lepers. This description of Jesus fits the Gospel Jesus. However, the giving of life to a clay bird is found in the *Arabic Gospel of the Infancy* (verse 36). Later, Christians would often deny that Muhammad was a genuine prophet because he did not perform miracles, although the *hadith* and *sira* describe some. Jesus preached that Allah was his Lord and Lord of his followers. Verse 79 denies that a prophet would ever have invited people to worship himself; Jesus only ever taught people to worship God. Jesus' likeness with God is the same as Adam's, which means that both had no human father. Most Muslims believe in Jesus' virgin birth. Why do Christians and Jews dispute with Muslims over Abraham, when neither the Book of Moses nor Jesus' Book existed until after Abraham, who was neither a Jew nor a Christian but a Muslim. Christians should join Muslims in affirming that there is One God and that God has no partners.

All, in fact, should follow the religion of Abraham. Yet Christians are not all alike. Some refrain from what is forbidden and practise what is permitted. This verse, 113, describes Christians in the exact words that 110 used to define the *ummah*.

Verse 115 says that God will reject nothing good that such Christians perform. Verse 84 affirms that all prophets are equal, that God makes no distinction between them. Esack (1997) argues that having criticized Jews and Christians for religious exclusiveness, it would be contradictory for the Qur'an to make a one-and-only claim for Islam. All who submit to God's will, he says, are Muslim and *din* refers to such people, not to "ethno-social membership of a particular group" (133). Some people of the book are condemned, but others are described as believers; Islam encourages the latter in their existing belief and invites the former to embrace belief. Anticipating 4: 157, which is widely taken to deny Jesus' crucifixion, verse 55 says that God raised Jesus to be with Himself to protect him from plots against him. Most Muslims believe that Jesus was raised up to heaven, from where he will return to earth before Judgement Day to die a natural death before sharing in the general resurrection, referred to in 55. Then, he will marry and raise a family. He will, according to *hadith*, kill the pigs, destroy crosses and aid in the defeat of the Evil One (Bukhari, 3: 425). This chapter, as has the whole of the Qur'an so far, stresses the importance of charity but reiterates that giving to the needy merely as a public display while nurturing evil in your heart is futile. Incidentally, verses 21 and 181, not unlike Jesus' Gospel reference to the slaying of prophets (Matthew 23: 37), rebuke the killing of God's messengers (see also 2: 87; 2: 91; 4: 155; 5: 70).

Some Much-Discussed Verses

Surah 4, "Women", continues to address the situation following Uhud and also contains significant verses for Christian–Muslim relations, including one of the most challenging, 4: 157. The deaths at Uhud left widows and orphans without guardians. The opening verse says that God created men and women from a single *nafs* (soul) and spouses for them of "like nature". Verse 2 calls for the restoration of property to orphans. Verse 3 permits men to marry up to four wives if they can treat them fairly; if, not, they should marry "only one". However, the provision here is to deal justly with orphans and widows. Some Muslims regard this as universally applicable; Islamic law has often recognized men's right to have four wives. Others regard this as provisional and contingent on circumstances similar to the post-Uhud context, arguing that the Qur'anic ideal is monogamy, suggested by verse 1, among other verses. Muslims have also interpreted this verse to allow unlimited concubines; others challenge this, arguing that those whom "your right hand possesses" (*Ma malakat aymanukum*) either includes concubines among the four or counts those of the "right hand" as "spouses" (Barlas, 270 n. 27). Wealthy guardians should seek no compensation for caring for orphans. Those who consume their inheritance will be consumed in the Fire. Verses 11 to 14 and also 176, the final verse, again deal with inheritance. While women receive two-thirds less than men, their right to inherit is guaranteed. Muslims often point out that as men are expected to maintain women, men require a larger share. This is made explicit at 34, where men are described as "protectors and maintainers of their wives" because God has preferred (*faddala*) men over women. Some interpret this to mean that God prefers men over women (Wadud, 71). Amina Wadud rejects the contention that either *daraja* at 2: 228 or this verse subordinates women to men. She applies "maintenance" to refer to husbands' responsibilities to care for their wives during pregnancy and child-rearing, which should be a partnership. This, she says, is linked with our "trusteeship of the earth" (73–4). Saeed (2008) uses different translations of 4: 34 to illustrate how a translator's views influence their choice of words. Surah 4: 34 says that if wives refuse to consent to sexual intercourse, husbands can "lightly beat them" (*'idribuhunna*). Some translate as "beat". Others annotate traditions limiting this to using a folded-up handkerchief or a toothbrush (131). Or, it can mean to "separate from" as at 57: 13, where a Wall (*faduriba*) separates the redeemed from the damned. Wadud argues that Islam prohibits wife-beating of any description. *Daraba* does not "necessarily indicate force or violence" but can mean striking out in a new direction. In this view, she says, instead of permitting wife-beating, which may have been a pre-Islamic practice, the verse actually condemns it (76).

Women own what they inherit or earn (verse 32) absolutely and are not required to contribute to their own maintenance or to the upkeep of the family. They may, of course, choose to do so. Wadud says there is no reason why women cannot provide for themselves since "whenever anyone performs tasks normally attributed to the other gender in addition to" their "own normal tasks, he or she will earn an additional reward". They will be raised in *darajah* (66–7). Reference to women keeping their earnings also means that Islam recognized their right to work. Arbitration rather than divorce is encouraged.

Four witnesses are required against the charge of adultery. Several verses deal with consanguinity. Verses 59, 69 and 80 again instruct believers to obey Muhammad, anticipating some important verses about Muhammad in Surah 33. Verse 59 also says that Muslims should obey those whom Muhammad deputized. Those who fight when the community is threatened are a "grade higher" (*darajah*) than those who stay at home. Even on the battlefield, prayer should be offered, with one party guarding another. Verse 43 allows clean sand to substitute for water when performing *wudu*.

Verse 82 says that if the Qur'an were not from God, it would contain some discrepancy. Muslims should always exchange a greeting with courtesy, although some Muslims reserve *AsSalamu Alakyum* for Muslims (86). There is, however, no warrant to respond to Christians with *samm alaykum* ('*poison be on you*') as some choose to do (Sonn, 260). Verses 97–8 express God's special concern for the weak and oppressed. People can fool their neighbours, says 108, but they can not hide their crimes from God. However, those who seek forgiveness from God will always receive forgiveness (110). Jesus is the main subject of verses 153 to 172. Jesus was God's servant (172), a spirit and a word from God whose followers commit excess by claiming that he was more than a messenger (171). Desist from calling Jesus God's son. God is one, not a Trinity. Verse 171 also calls Jesus Messiah; the Arabic here is a title of respect, like "master" (Parrinder, 33). When the Jews claim to have crucified Jesus, they did not. Rather, it appeared to them as if they had. Non-Muslims have detected Docetic and Gnostic influence here. A popular Muslim belief is that Judas was crucified in Jesus' place, while God rescued Jesus by raising him to Himself (4: 158; 3: 55). Yet Jesus will die, so Christians are those who believe in Jesus *before his death* (4: 159). On Judgement Day, Jesus will be a witness against them. Jesus' birth and works are similar in the Qur'an and Gospels; however, the "end" of his life is different.

Analysis

The migration, verses that permit self-defence and armed struggle against oppression, Muhammad's role as political and military leader in addition to his spiritual authority, the five pillars and some legal material were discussed in this chapter. Muhammad was no dictator, however, but was instructed to consult before taking a decision. What we might call Islam's version of the gospel was also summarized. Chapter 4, which takes us to the end of the sequence of revelation, picks up at Surah 33. Gender and war will continue to be important issues. Chapter 4, as it traces Muhammad's career from 627 until his death, including the fall of Mecca and the last pilgrimage, picks up the sequence at 33 and continues to ground content in context.

The Community Consolidates 4

The Battle of the Trench

We begin with the Battle of the Trench and end with the most probable last revelations. Surah 33 is called "The Confederates". These were the anti-Muslim allies whose troops, numbering 10,000, marched against the Muslims, who numbered about 3,000, in March 617. Among the Confederates were members of a Jewish tribe, the Banu al-Nadir, who had been expelled from Medina after Uhud, when the tribe's elders had challenged Muhammad's leadership or were plotting to kill him (Lings, 203). The Banu Qaynuqa had been expelled earlier for breaking the covenant (Lings, 161). As news of the advancing enemy army led by Abu Sufyan reached Medina, Salman al-Farsi advised that in Persia, when threatened by attack, they built a defensive trench around their cities. Salman not only devised the strategy but "knew exactly how wide and how deep the trench would have to be" (Lings, 216). Muhammad himself worked all day helping to construct the fortifications, which took six days to prepare. Several miracles are mentioned in the *sira*, such as removing a large rock by spitting on it, which pulverized it (Guillaume, 451) and causing a few dates placed on a garment to multiply into enough to feed all the workers (452). Some very significant verses in this *surah* relate to Muhammad's wives. Since migrating to Medina, Muhammad had married Umar's daughter Hafsa, a widow (his fourth marriage) (February 625), a cousin's widow called Zainab whose husband had died at Badr (March 625; his fifth marriage) and Salama, whose husband had died at Uhud (his sixth marriage). Zainab died several months after marrying Muhammad. Muhammad's seventh marriage was to another Zainab, previously married to his adopted son, Zayd, which exceeded the four wives permitted by 4: 3. Verses in Surah 33 deal specifically with this marriage, which took place in the same year as the Battle of the Trench. The Battle, or siege, waged for 25 nights (Lings, 229). Both sides suffered light fatalities, about six Muslims and three of the enemy (Guillaume, 469). Another Jewish tribe, the Banu Qurayza, colluded with the Confederates, weakening the city's defences on the south-east where the Quraza's own fortress lay. The Confederates, however, could not sustain the siege; the wind was against them and they and their horses and camels began to starve. They had neither food nor water. Ibn Kathir says that "Allah sent cold winds with strong gusts against the Confederates, and they were left with no tents or anything else" (Ibn Kathir, vol. 7, p. 647). The oasis of Medina, with plenty of water, was protected from the winds. The result was a victory for the Muslims; the Confederacy itself broke apart.

Surah 33 has 73 verses, beginning with "O Prophet, do not listen to the unbelievers or to the hypocrites. It is God who is all knowing and full of wisdom". Muhammad is to be guided by what comes to him as inspiration, trusting God completely to order his affairs. Verses 4–5 declare that adopted sons should be called by the names of their biological fathers, not by the names of their adoptive father. This applied to Zayd, which also meant that Zayd's wife, if he divorced her, would not be ruled out as a partner for Muhammad by the rules of consanguinity (4: 23). Actually, this only applied to natural sons but there was a "strong social principle not to make a distinction between sons by birth and sons by adoption" (Lings, 213).

Zayd's marriage with Zainab was not happy, and he was also aware that Zainab loved Muhammad, as he did. It was, according to Lings, Zayd who approached Muhammad announcing his intent to divorce her. Initially, Muhammad discouraged this (Lings, 213). Non-Muslims have long regarded verse 5 as an example of Muhammad manufacturing revelation for his own purposes; Muir had it that Muhammad married Zainab before this verse was revealed then pre-empted scandal by "falling back on the Oracle" with verse 37 specifically sanctioning the marriage. Muir has it that the "absolute ascendancy of" Muhammad's "powerful mind over" the community was strong enough to remove the scandal (1912, 291–2). Verse 38 says that it was Muhammad's duty to take care of Zainab. By marrying her, he not only raised her to the dignity of becoming a Mother of the Believers but also rescued her from an unhappy situation. Verse 50 means that it was "not obligatory" for Muhammad "to divide his time equally between his wives" (Ibn Kathir, vol. 8, p. 19). This appears to exempt Muhammad from the requirement of 4: 3 to treat all wives equally, to "do justice to them". Yet his life as Prophet and their lives as his wives placed heavy responsibilities on all of them. For Muhammad to enjoy some freedom in how he organized his domestic affairs was a mercy and a blessing. More will be said about Muhammad's multiple marriages in the Conclusion.

Verse 6 describes Muhammad as closer to Muslims than they are themselves, and his wives as their Mothers. Verse 36 says that once Muhammad had made a decision, people must not dispute this. However, 3: 159 and 42: 38 require prior consultation. Verse 40 declares that he is indeed God's messenger and the seal (*khatam*) of all the prophets. This is one of four verses that uses Muhammad's actual name (see also 3: 144; 47: 2; 48: 29). From this, Muslims conclude that Muhammad is the final prophet, whose Book is the last testament. Even in the midst of battle, Muhammad is described as a bringer of good news and a warner. Peace is the ultimate aim; in paradise, the believers will exchange the "peace be on you" greeting. Verse 56 instructs believers to bless Muhammad's name when they speak by adding "peace be on him" (*Sallallahu Alaihi wa Sallam*). In fact, Muslims honour all prophets in this manner. Ali comments on how Muhammad's wives played significant roles in the community. The two Zainabs "devoted themselves to the poor". Others, as did Muhammad's daughter, Fatimah, tended the sick. Some carried water on the battlefield. They trained other women in "social work" (1053). The Mothers of the Believers occupy an honourable place in Muslim memory. Verse 9 refers to the wind that God had sent against the besieging Confederates. The Muslims had been besieged by a great force, which had tested them so that a "great shaking" occurred. Hypocrites failed the test and started rumours that the enemy had breached the trench and were raiding their homes as they camped out "in the space between the City and the Trench" (Ali, 1059 n. 3684). Declaring that despite all his promises, Muhammad had merely deluded them they wanted to abandon post and return to protect their homes. This, says verse 15, would have broken the Covenant they had entered, which recognized Muhammad's authority. They would gain nothing by running away. One of the enemy did cross the Trench, but Ali defeated him in hand-to-hand combat (Ibn Kathir, vol. 7, p. 648). Others are condemned for contributing nothing to defending the community then bragging that it was their deeds that had saved the day. Those who were eager to protect their properties had hearts set on worldly affairs. Verse 21 describes Muhammad's *sunnah* as a beautiful, or noble (*hasan*) example. It is this declaration that would give so much importance in Islam to the *hadith*, accounts of what Muhammad said and did. In later years, the *sunnah* served as the second most authoritative source for Islamic practice, customs, norms and laws. Lings describes a bench outside the Prophet's mosques on which the destitute sat (167). They may have been voluntarily poor, the pioneers of Sufi Islam, thus they were the *Ahl-as-Suffah*, people of the Bench, although "Sufi" is also said to be from the woollen (*s. ūf*) clothes they wore and from *s. afā* (purity). Others suggest that some sat there to be close to Muhammad, to record *hadith*. Despite their strength of number, God turned the polytheists and their allies away. Those who aided them, the Qurayza, were to be punished. After the siege, the Qurayza retreated to their fortress and shut themselves in, aware that they had broken the Covenant. During the siege, aware of their treachery, Muhammad had sent a message reminding them of their treaty obligations. Their fortress was attacked and defeated. Muhammad appointed the leader of another Jewish tribe, who had acted as an envoy to them during the siege, to determine their fate, which he did. The men were to be executed and their families and property seized. This, says Lings, "corresponded exactly with Jewish law", citing Deuteronomy 20: 12 (Lings, 232). Non-Muslims tend to single out the attack on the Qurayzi as an act of unjustified violence and brutality; Muir comments that this act removed the last "remnant of opposition, political or religious, from the immediate neighborhood of Medina". Although, he wrote, "the bloody deed did not escape … hostile criticism" it "struck so great a terror into the hearts of all … that no one dared openly impugn it" (322).

Gender Relations

A cluster of important verses address Muhammad's wives. Non-Muslims often represent the so-called Zayd–Zainab affair as proof of Muhammad's lust and lack of sexual restraint, supposedly marrying at will whomsoever he wanted to possess. Verse 52, though, says that Muhammad was not to marry again. Ali says that he did not do so after this except for Mary the Copt, who was presented as a gift from the Archbishop of Alexandria in Egypt. Mary gave him a son, Ibrahim, who predeceased Muhammad (Ali, 1074 n. 3754). However, Muhammad did marry Juwairia in January 627, Umm Habiba, Abu Sufyan's daughter, in late 627 or early 628, Safiyah in 628, and Maimunah in 629. Mary the Copt was presented in 630. All are counted among the Mothers of the Believers. Verse 53 says that people should not enter the quarters of Muhammad's wives until invited. People were taking liberties, entering unbidden and outstaying their welcome. According to Ibn Kathir, this verse was revealed during Zainab's wedding feast. Muhammad retired during the feast, then returned to the room expecting to find that the guests had left when he had. However, they were still present, so he hung a curtain (*hijab*) between the remaining guests and his wives (Bukhari, 65: 374). Umar may already have suggested this practice (Ibn Kathir, vol. 8, p. 23). The wives are only to show their faces before relatives (55). This is taken to mean that they should wear *hijab* in public, a cloth covering their faces. Ibn Abbas attributes another aspect of this verse, which prohibits the wives of Muhammad from remarrying after his death, to a request from a companion for Aisha's hand following the Prophet's death (Ibn Kathir, vol. 8, p. 45). These verses clearly address the Mothers of the Believers. They are instructed to stay quietly in their quarters, to wear modest dress, to pray, give to charity and to obey Muhammad. They are also described as members of the Family of the Prophet or people of the House (*ahlu-al-bayt*), who must be "pure and spotless". The Family included Fatimah, Ali and their two sons, Hasan and Husayn. Shia regard this special status afforded to the Prophet's family to indicate that his descendants would have a unique claim to lead the community. They must not hanker for worldly possessions or attract scandal of any kind, which might refer to an incident concerning Aisha which we discuss later in this chapter. Muhammad was authorized to set any wife free who did not wish to serve as an example and inspiration to the whole community. They are unlike other women, so will receive double reward for righteousness and double punishment for wrongdoing.

Two remaining verses, 35 and 59, require comment. Verse 35 says that Allah will reward the prayers, charity, fasting, chastity and righteousness of believing men and of believing women. There is no indication here of what some argue is a Qur'anic preference for men. Wadud, among others, argues that the Qur'an never distinguishes men as more valuable than women, although it does recognize biological difference. Indeed, she writes, "every usage of the masculine plural form is intended to include males and females, *equally*" (4) and likewise verses which specifically refer to women also address men (98). Just as the Qur'an did not prohibit slavery but gave a strong indication that it should be abolished (see 2: 177; 4: 92; 90: 13), so the Qur'anic principles of equality and justice point to complete legal as well as spiritual gender equality (Wadud, 101). This helps to introduce verse 59, which advises or instructs Muhammad's wives and believing women to wrap themselves in their cloak (*jilbab*) when in public, to identify them as Muslim women. This became the basis for the legal requirement, in some Muslim countries, that women cover their faces or even their whole bodies when outside their homes, accompanied by a male relative. Ibn Kathir cites

Ibn Abbas that 33: 59 required women to cover themselves in public; "Allah commanded the believing women, when they went out of their homes for some need, to cover their faces from above their heads with the *jilbab*, leaving only one eye showing." Wadud, Ahmed and others, including al-Ghazali, refute this requirement. Ahmed says that during Muhammad's lifetime, only Muhammad's wives wore *hijab*, so that the expression "taking the *hijab*" (*darabat al-hijab*) was a synonym for marrying him (1992, 53–4). Wadud regards such verses as equally applicable to men; neither men nor women should engage in "wanton display" (98). Linked with 24: 30, modest dress is indeed a cross-gender requirement. Al-Ghazali takes the surprising view that it contradicts Islam to compel women to cover their faces. There is, he pointed out, no requirement to do so at prayer or during the pilgrimage, thus, "how could Islam ask women to cover their faces at ordinary times?" Those who claim, he says, that "women's reform is conditional on wearing the veil are lying to God and his prophet" (Afkhami, 71). Muslim women are actually commanded not to imitate the Mothers of the Believers.

The Trench to the Treaty

Our sequence gives 60 as the next *surah*. However, this is probably from after the Treaty of Hudaybiyah and will be discussed later. Surah 4 is next, which we have already paraphrased. Zarkash then lists 99, 57, 47, 13, 55, 76, 65, 98, 59, 110 then 24. Surah 24 can be dated between the Battle of the Trench and before the Treaty (March 628). Surah 57 may be later, after 630. Ali thinks that Surahs 99 and 47 were earlier. He thinks that 65 is probably from around AH 6. Surah 59 has material related to the expulsion of the Banu al-Nadir, but there is no reason to date its appearance earlier than the period we are now discussing. Ali identifies 55 and 76 as Meccan, with some passages from Medina. Although the earlier date could be accurate, we leave these *surahs* where Zarkash placed them. Surah 110, however, is almost certainly one of the last passages revealed, so will be summarized towards the end of this chapter. Few external events provide specific context here, but this sequence continues to illustrate how the *ummah* was consolidating as a social-religious-political community, or nation.

With eight short, concise verses, Surah 99, while "generally referred to the early Madinah period" could be from Mecca (Ali, 1680). The title, "Earthquake", is from the opening verse, which begins "when the earth shudders" and "convulses". On that day, the smallest good and the tiniest bad deed will be counted. The twenty verses of Surah 57 begin with the heavens and earth praising God. The title, "Iron", refers to a word in verse 25; God gave us *hadid*, which has many uses. This *surah* contains some important theology; God is immanent and transcendent, omnipotent and omniscient. Creator of everything, everything will return to God. Verse 4 describes God as firmly established on God's throne. This and other verses that suggest that God has human characteristics will be discussed in my Conclusion. Through Muhammad, God leads people from darkness into light. In verse 10, a reference to "The Victory" might indicate a date after the conquest of Mecca, although Ali suggests a "general meaning" that those who struggle in God's cause are always worthy (1422 n. 5286). The light motif surfaces again when hypocrites, on Judgement Day, will ask believers to share their light with them. Instead, a Wall (faduriba; related to the word translated as "beat" at 4: 34) will separate believers from the hypocrites. This has been identified as the Record of our own deeds (Ali, 1423 n. 5291). People lead themselves into temptation. No ransom will be accepted on that day. Those who give to charity, act righteously and struggle in God's cause are raised above those who lag behind at times of crisis. The former are a light to others. Enjoying this world at the cost of spiritual health is like a plant that thrives briefly then withers away. Verse 27 describes the Christian practice of priestly and monastic celibacy as an innovation which God did not command. People of the Book may claim that their religion is the only path to God but God is not answerable to them.

Surah 47 honours Muhammad, after whom it is named. Only eight other *surahs* are named after individuals. Pickthall contextualizes verse 18 as a reference to Muhammad looking back on Mecca, his beloved city, as he left in 622 and weeping. Verse 4 describes fighting as a test of faith. The expression "strike at their necks" indicates, says Ali, that when fighting from necessity this must be conducted with complete resolve; "you cannot wage war with kid gloves" but must attack the enemy where they are most vulnerable (1315 n. 4820). We are once more invited to travel the earth to see what befell the unrepentant. Satan does succeed in turning some away from the true path. Others become faint-hearted when a *surah* calling for struggle or even armed resistance is revealed. Yet those who apostatize and corrupt others cannot harm God. Sometimes, fighting evil must take priority over peace. God is above all need; God can replace Muslims with another people if they fail God. Verse 38 says that misers are miserly at the cost of their own souls.

Surah 13, called "Thunder", has 43 verses. It begins with cryptic letters.

The "thunder" refers to verse 13, which says that even thunder and lightning praise God, indeed they blaze God's praise. We again learn that God is firmly established on God's Throne. Eveything obeys God's laws. Unbelievers constantly demand a sign – a recurring motif – yet signs surround them in nature. God's angels record our hidden and public thoughts. Taking other, false gods as protectors is futile. In comparison with the true God, they are blind and consigned to darkness. They created nothing. The wicked will still be condemned even if they could ransom the entire earth. Verse 20 uses "covenant" (*mithaq*) for the *ummah*–God relationship, which is unusual. Other passages speak of God's covenant with Israel (2: 40; 2: 83–4; 2: 93 for example) and with the prophets (3: 81; 33: 7–8). To keep the covenant, Muslims are to pray, give to charity, repel evil and join with God only what God demands (see also 41: 34). Muslims have permission to fight injustice, but winning the argument is always the better strategy. Heaven waits for those who persevere in patience where angels will greet them with the "peace". The Qur'an has sufficient power to split mountains, yet the hard of heart resist its sublime message. Verse 30 says that God provides wives for the prophets. Marriage is regarded as a duty in Islam. This is why popular belief has it that Jesus will marry when he returns, since in traditional accounts Jesus was unmarried. Revealed in Arabic to Arabs, the Qur'an is clear and easy to understand. Verse 42 relates to the plot to kill or capture Muhammad on the eve of the *hijrah*, which God foiled.

Surah 55 has 78 verses. The title, "Al Rahman", or "the merciful", is taken from verse 1. God created humanity, gifting us with speech. God teaches through the Qur'an. A rhythmic *surah*, this is closer to Meccan passages in content and style. Regardless of issues about linguistic development, the longer Medina passages are more prosaic due to their pragmatic content. The Balance awaits us on Judgement Day. We should balance work and worship, work and leisure. We should give measure for measure in business. God created *jinns* from fire, people from clay. Again we have ships sailing the seas as a sign of divine mercy. Neither people nor *jinns* will need to account for their deeds on that day because records already exist. Our destiny is marked on our forelocks. Familiar descriptions of heaven and hell, including the presence of chaste youths in the former, follow before the *surah* concludes with a salutation to God, who is bountiful. Applying Wadud's exegesis, we can assume that the promised youths are of both sexes! The 76th *surah* is called "Humanity" and has 31 verses. God created us from sperm, gifting sight and hearing, says verse 2, adding "hearing" to "speech" as at 55: 4. God has made

God's way known to us, but many reject this. Familiar descriptions of heaven and hell also follow, adding the detail that heaven's residents will wear green silk clothes. Green was Muhammad's favourite colour, and is the colour of Islam. Surah 2: 138 says that no one can colour as God colours. Believers should celebrate God's name in the morning, during the evening and at night. Patience is necessary because the Qur'an descends gradually. God forgives at God's will, but it is the acts of the wicked that determine their destinies.

Surah 65, "Divorce", has 12 verses. Passages have already dealt with divorce. This *surah* introduced a new rule, possibly in response to a "mistake made by Umar in divorcing his wife" (Pickthall, 632). Umar divorced his wife when she was menstruating. He was then ordered to "take her back and keep her" until her period was over, then to wait until her next period was over before making the divorce final if he chose to do so (Ibn Kathir, vol. 10, p. 33). Two witnesses are now required to complete *talaq*. *Talaq* refers to male-initiated divorce, which does not require petitioning a judge but which does involve witnesses. Female-initiated divorce, which involves petitioning a court, is called *khul'u*. The mechanism is different, but Muslim feminists argue that rights and the goal are the same. Surah 2: 231 said that husbands could either retain their wives or 'let them go' during the waiting period, though they must not injure them. Surah 65: 6 says that women are entitled to wait in the home, with the same living conditions as their husband. Wadud sums up the Qur'anic teaching on marriage:

> The Qur'an prefers that men and women marry (4: 25). Within marriage, there should be harmony (4: 128) mutually built with love and mercy (30: 21). The marriage tie is considered protection for both the male and the female ... However, the Qur'an does not rule out the possibility of difficulty, which it suggests can be resolved. If all else fails, it also permits equitable divorce. (78)

Incidentally, the statement that marriage (*nikhat*) is a type of non-religious contract is nonsense; marriage in Islam is a profoundly sacred tying of two spouses together in a loving relationship. Sex is a divine gift, and a form of worship before which etiquette encourages prayer. Verses 8 to 12 change subject-matter, repeating the promise of paradise for the righteous and the certainty of punishment for the wicked.

Surah 98 has 8 verses. Named "Clear Evidence" after a reference in verse 1 to the clarity of God's revelation, the passage mainly addresses Christians and polytheists who reject the truth or create schism. Hellfire is waiting for them. Surah 59, called "Exile", has 24 verses. Exile here refers to the banishing of the Banu al-Nadir. Treachery backfires because the faithful only increase their resolve. The Banu al-Nadir were lucky; others have been punished more severely. The Qurayza retreated in fear to their fortress but could not escape God's wrath. Verse 6 refers to the Battle of the Trench, when neither camels nor horses were required to defeat the enemy. Verse 9 mentions destitute Muhajirs who, expelled from their homes, needed refuge as well as financial compensation. The Ansars who assisted them, embracing them as if they were siblings, were true Muslims. Some hypocrites even promise to assist those who are expelled for treason but lie; they have no intention of helping. The Qurayzi lacked courage to fight in the open. If the Qur'an had descended on a mountain top, the mountain would split apart (verse 21; similar to 13: 31); it contains parables; we should reflect on these and humble ourselves before God. The last two verses contain at least ten Beautiful Names. We are reminded that the gift of colour comes to us from the greatest artist of all.

Aisha, a Necklace and the Treaty

The Quraysh were inciting the Bani-I-Muttaliq to attack Mecca from their base on the Red Sea. In what might be described as a pre-emptive attack, before the end of 627 Muhammad led his troops to deal with this threat. The context is wider animosity between Mecca and Medina, that is, an ongoing war. Muhammad was accompanied by two wives, one of whom was Aisha, often described as his favourite. The clan was defeated. However, by marrying the chief's daughter, Juwayrihah, the survivors became Muhammad's kin-by-marriage so were subsequently freed without ransom (Lings, 242). During the return journey, Aisha became separated from the caravan when she went off to look for her necklace, which had slipped its chain. Left behind, she was found by Safwan, whom she knew from before "the veil was imposed", who escorted her to the camp (Lings, 241). When she reached Medina, Aisha fell ill and did not leave her quarters for "some twenty days" (Lings, 244). When she did, she discovered that a rumour was circulating that she and Safwan had committed adultery. Investigating the allegation, Muhammad found no evidence and defended the accused from the pulpit of the mosque. However, the scandal continued. He hoped for a revelation confirming innocence or guilt. None came. Aisha herself thought her case "too paltry to be spoken of in the Koran". Then Surah 24 came, in which her innocence was established, the penalties for adultery and also for false accusations of adultery were prescribed, and several verses of outstanding depth and beauty, too, were revealed. Aisha witnessed the revelation, which caused Muhammad to drip pearls of sweat (Bukhari, *48: 829*). Muhammad recited in a joyful voice (Lings, 245). Called "The Light", Surah 24 has 64 verses. It launches immediately into the subject-matter of adultery and fornication, declaring that those found guilty be given a hundred lashes. Once found guilty, a man or a woman can only marry a non-believer. Pious men are for pious women and vice versa; the unchaste are for the unchaste. The requirement for four witnesses can be substituted by five solemn oaths, both by the prosecutor and by the defendant. Those who accuse others unjustly are liable to be given 80 lashes. The charge against Aisha was a great lie. Scandalmongers will be punished on Judgement Day. Such people are cursed in this life and in the next.

A cluster of verses deal with aspects of *adat*, that is, etiquette or correct behaviour. There is a link here with Surah 33; Muslims should not enter believers' homes uninvited (see verses 22, 61; men and women should dress modestly and lower their gaze, which suggests that all Muslim women did not wear the veil (30–1)). If they did, there would be no need for men to lower their gaze. Marriage, the *surah* suggests, is a grace from God. Older women can put their cloaks aside (60). The unmarried must remain chaste; God will give people a means to find a partner. God, says verse 35, is the light of the heavens and the earth. *Al-Nur* is a Beautiful Name. Allah guides us to God's light. This light, like a brilliant star, is housed in a niche fed with eternal oil from a Tree that belongs to neither East nor West. This is a parable for men and women. When the *mihrab* (used at 19: 11) became a feature of mosques, marking the *qiblah*, based on this parable a light is often included. Nor is this imagery the only sublime example of Qur'anic language contained in this chapter; we also read that the deeds of the wicked are as insubstantial as a mirage in the desert of God creating some creatures that creep on their bellies, some that walk on two, some on four legs. Several verses reiterate Muhammad's authority declaring that everyone will be treated justly by him (47, 50–4, 62–3). His only duty is to preach the message clearly. He will establish Islam for his people, the religion that God has chosen. Muslims worship no God but God and obey Muhammad.

The Treaty of Hudaybiyah

The treaty represents a seminal moment, a triumph in Islam almost as important as the Fall of Mecca. In February 628, Muhammad and pilgrims set out to perform the pilgrimage. Wearing the seamless white pilgrim's dress, Muhammad was accompanied by 1,400 men (Pickthall, xiii). There were 70 camels for sacrifice (Guillaume, 500). Muhammad camped at "the declivity of al-Hudaybiya below Mecca" and sent a peace-envoy to inform the Quraysh that he did not want to fight but to perform his sacred duty. Muhammad and the pilgrims were unarmed. Uthman, who later became the third Caliph, was related to Abu Sufyan and so might be well received, acted as chief envoy. Rumour reached the Muslims' camp that he had been murdered. This proved false, but a party of Quraysh left Mecca intent on attacking the Muslim camp. They were captured, taken to Muhammad and forgiven. The Quraysh responded by sending "proper envoys" who negotiated a treaty, which was to remain in force for ten years. Hostilities would cease. The terms were somewhat favourable to the Qurayshi; "deserters from the Quraysh to the Muslims were to be returned" but not vice versa. Muhammad would not be permitted to enter Mecca that year (Pickthall, xii–xiii). Some Muslims were critical of the treaty but it proved to be a victory, celebrated by Surah 48. Between the signing of the Treaty and the Fall of Mecca, more people became Muslim than "the total number of all previous converts" and the two sides now "met and talked together" (Pickthall, xiii).

Shortly after returning to Medina, an attack took place on Muhammad's life. A Jewish sorcerer, bribed by the tribe of Khaybar which opposed Islam, placed a spell on him. Muhammad's memory started to fail and he became very weak. Realizing that some sorcery was in play, he recited the verses of refuge (Surah 113 and 114) and recovered. With the threat from Mecca removed by the peace, he set out to deal with Khaybar, which appeared to be impregnably fortified. Then Muhammad learned about an underground stream that could enable the fort to endure a siege indefinitely. Blocking this, the troops soon grew thirsty and were driven to "come out and fight". The Muslims won after a "savage battle" (Lings, 266–7). It was after Khaybar that Muhammad married Safiyah, the widow of the defeated chief. This cemented a peace between the Muslims and the subjugated tribe. At Khaybar, however, he ate some meat that had been deliberately poisoned. He forgave the woman responsible when she said she had tried to poison him because of "the humili-ation of her people" (Pickthall, xiii). It was this illness that eventually led to his death. *Hadith* have the meat warning Muhammad before he actually swallowed what was in his mouth (Guillaume, 516). It was at this time that the emigrants returned from Ethiopia. The next year, 629, Muhammad performed *Umrah*, accompanied by 2,000 pilgrims. The Quraysh more or less evacuated the city for the duration of the pilgrimage. He completed the seven circuits of the Ka'bah, passed to and from between Safa and Marwah, sacrificed a camel and had his head shaved. Muhammad wanted to enter the Ka'bah, despite the presence of idols, but was denied access on the grounds that this was not specified by the Treaty (Lings, 281). He was also denied permission to remain beyond the stipulated three days to celebrate his marriage to Maimunah, a widowed relative. In September 629, following the murder of an envoy across the Byzantine border, Muhammad led a force of 3,000 against the offending city of Muta. First, Muhammad invited the citizens to embrace Islam. Battle followed. Then reinforcements came to augment the Byzantine troops, which may have exceeded 100,000, forcing a Muslim retreat (Guillaume, 532).

We now turn to a cluster of *surahs* from this period, with 57 as an anchor. Following Zarkash and skipping 22, which we have already discussed, we move through 63, 58, 49, 66, 61, 62, 64 to 48. We conclude with 110, 5 and 9. Surah 63, says Ali, is one of "ten short Madinah Surahs dealing with a special feature in the social life" of the *ummah* (1470). This fits our concern with how the community was consolidating its identity, norms and ethos. The title, "Hypocrites", from verse 1, suggests that the unity of the community was a major issue. Some bear witness that Muhammad is God's Messenger, which is the first *fard* (obligatory) duty but they lie. God has sealed their hearts; they may appear pious and righteous externally but internally they are as rotten timber. They even sneer secretly at the Prophet, begging his forgiveness while smirking on the other side of their face. We may, if we wish, pray for their souls but their hypocrisy has sealed their fate. Our riches, our families, nothing of this world, should deflect us from remembrance (*Dhikr*) of God. Surah 58 has 22 verses. Called "She Who Pleads", the title refers to a woman who carries her anguish to God when dealt with unjustly. A man could declare that his wife was to him as his "mother" (*zihar*) then cease to have marital relations with her, often also neglecting her welfare. Verse 2 declares that no one can be our mother except our biological mothers. If a Muslim does pronounce *zihar*, he cannot take his wife back without freeing a slave, fasting for two months or feeding 60 destitute people. Ali suggests that if no penalty were imposed, men would resort to this too readily (1433 n. 5335). With almost all verses stipulating a penalty, Muslims are told not to transgress limits (*hudud*). More will be said about this below. Muslims are warned against meeting in secret counsel, excluding Muhammad. Giving to charity is recommended before a private audience with the Prophet. As for hypocrites, neither their riches nor their sons will profit them on Judgement Day. All who resist Allah and God's messenger will be humiliated. No one who does not love God and Muhammad will enter paradise. God strengthens all believers with God's spirit.

Surah 49, called "The Chambers", is 18 verses long. Ali dates this from after the Conquest of Mecca, during what is known as the "year of deputations", but we will paraphrase it here, since its theme of respect for Muhammad's leadership is relevant. Following the Treaty, Muhammad began writing to other rulers, inviting them to embrace Islam. He signed himself "Apostle of God". He wrote to the ruler of Ethiopia, to the Byzantine Emperor and to the Shah of Iran, among others. Called to be the universal prophet, he knew that Islam was to be offered to all humanity. Believers should not raise their voices above Muhammad's, or shout out from behind his inner quarters, which gives the name of the *surah* (verse 4). Again, this deals with etiquette. The *ummah* is a single community, so peace and reconciliation is always best. Disputes should be adjudicated justly. Sarcasm, laughing at those we think are less capable or worthy than ourselves, calling people offensive names, spying on each other and defaming others are proscribed. To our surprise, we may find that we are objects of laughter at the Judgement Day. God made us from a single soul, and gave us spouses. He made us into nations and tribes so that we might learn about and benefit from our racial and cultural diversity. Here, the Qur'an affirms both racial equality and the value of all cultures. Some who embrace Islam even think they do God a favour. The reverse is true; Islam is God's favour to humanity. Surah 66, with 12 verses, is called "Prohibition". This *surah* may address some jealousy within the Prophet's Household. Aisha is said to have asked Muhammad who would be counted among his wives in paradise (Lings, 271). On one occasion, perhaps referred to in verse 3, the wives sent Fatimah to her father on their behalf asking him to deal with Aisha's behaviour. In response, Muhammad said, "trouble me not with regard to Aishah, for verily revelation cometh not unto me when I am beneath the coverlet of a wife, except that wife be 'Aishah" (Lings, 272). Muhammad spent what other wives thought was too much time with one wife, whom he presented with a gift of honey, which he himself loved, so they devised a scheme that allowed them to express their displeasure. When Muhammad came to their quarters, they told him that his breath smelt. He intensely disliked bad smells. Subsequently, he declared he would never eat honey again. Verse 1 picks up here, telling Muhammad not to prohibit what God permits. When Muhammad confides in his wives, they must not divulge this confidence. Verse 5 speaks to all the wives; they should behave with all decorum because Muhammad had God's permission to divorce them and to marry other women in their place. The motif of believers as a light resurfaces at verse 8. Our lights will illuminate our paths. God will perfect our Light and admit us into paradise. The wives and mothers of past prophets provide models for women today, including Mary who was a faithful servant, into whom God breathed God's spirit.

Surahs 61 and 62 are called "The Ranks" and "Friday". Respectively, they have 14 and 11 verses. The name of 61 is from verse 3, which says that God loves to see believers side by side in solidarity, as if ready for battle. Verse 61 has Jesus predicting that "Ahmed" (the diminutive for Muhammad) would follow him as God's prophet. Yet when Muhammad appeared, he was accused of being a sorcerer. Evil aims to extinguish God's Light but God has sent Islam as the religion of truth, over all "religion". This can be interpreted as a one-and-only claim or as a condemnation of false religion. Verse 14 describes Jesus' disciples as God's helpers, or servants. Surah 62 emphasizes that prayer is central to the *ummah*'s life. God sent Muhammad, who is unlettered, to the lettered and unlettered alike. Previous people of the Book became steeped in ignorance; like a donkey carrying a load of books which he cannot read they failed to keep their covenant. Those who think they are saved to the exclusion of others should welcome death; instead, they fear death because they know that their deeds will condemn them. When the believers gather for the Friday congregational prayer, mandatory for men they should forget about business and all that distracts them, praising Allah and centring on Allah's worship. Nor should they hurry off as soon as prayer ends. They should patiently wait to share the peace, with which *salat* ends. Surah 64 is called "Mutual Disillusion" or "Loss and Gain" and has 18 verses. Ali says that all of these shorter Medinan *surahs* deal with some aspect of the life of the community (Ali, 1475). The title is from verse 9. At Judgement, some who think they are saved will find themselves hell-bound, while some who thought they were damned will find themselves in paradise; some will "lose" what others "gain". Again, the community is instructed to obey Muhammad (verses 8 and 12), whose Book is Light from God. Our families may sometimes be a test of our faith; as God forgives us, so we should be forgiving towards members of our family when they annoy us or misbehave. Family as the basic unit of society is precious in Islam, the nursery where we are schooled in love of God and in love for all God's creatures.

In early January 630, allies of the Quraysh broke the Treaty by attacking a clan that was allied with the Muslims. Surah 60, or "She who is to be Examined", is dated soon after the breach of the Treaty but before the Conquest of Mecca, although verse 12 fits the Conquest context (see below). Friendship is a major motif, which Surah 5 will continue. Enemies must not be taken as friends. Similarly, 3: 28 says that believers should not befriend unbelievers. Yet God can transform our enemies into friends, replacing hostility with mutual love. Surah 41: 34 had said that Muslims should always try to overcome hostility with friendship, so that those who hate us become our friends. Abraham is a model for all believers; his example, like Muhammad's is *uswa hasana*, except when he prayed forgiveness for his father because, as an idolater, his father had sealed his own fate. Neither relatives nor friends can help us before God. This brings us to Surah 48, entitled "The Victory" (*fath*). *Fath* is related to the word "opening" that names Surah 1. The same word would be used for the wars of conquest that followed Muhammad's death. The Victory was the Treaty of Hudaybiyah, but the conquest of Mecca is foreshadowed. Given the increase in the size of the *ummah*, Muhammad was able to lead a force of 10,000 men towards Mecca. Aware that Muhammad now led an overwhelmingly superior force, Abu Sufyan sued for peace. Reluctantly, Abu Sufyan embraced Islam and an amnesty was agreed; all who stayed in their homes, or took refuge in Abu Sufyan's home or in the mosque, would be spared. A handful of implacable, unrepentant enemies who had also committed either murder or treason were executed. Several people initially condemned were pardoned. Abu Jahl's son converted, saying he would work twice as hard in Islam's service as he had worked to defeat Islam. Hind, Abu Sufyan's wife, was one of the last to convert. The way in which Muhammad invited her to embrace Islam closely follows 60: 12; he said that she must not commit adultery, steal, slander others or kill her children. She replied that she was only guilty of taking a little of Abu Sufyan's money to buy food with because he was a miser. As for her children, she had raised them but the Muslims had slain them at Badr (Guillaume, 553). Declaring that truth has come, so falsehood should be destroyed (Surah 17: 81), Muhammad entered the Ka'bah and toppled the idols, some 360 of them, ordering that they be broken into pieces except for an image or icon of Mary and child and one of Abraham, which he preserved (Lings, 300). This may suggest that Islam is not totally opposed to "icons" although it strongly favours non-representational art.

Al-Fath has 29 verses, of which the final verse is one of the longest in the Qur'an. The Treaty is declared to be a great Victory, a triumph. It indicates God's favour. Having sent peace and tranquillity into their hearts, he has also supported them with heavenly hosts. The blind and the disabled have no need for an excuse but those who drag their feet or who desert their posts to take booty have cause to fear God's wrath. Nor is it an excuse to say that we have flocks to shepherd when the defence and survival of the community is at stake. How courageous it had been for the unarmed band of Muslims to attempt the *hajj*. It was God who honoured their faith by restraining the hands of the enemy. Muhammad would enter the Sacred Mosque: he would complete the ritual of *hajj*; he would shave his hair and honour Abraham and Abraham's God. Muhammad is God's messenger and those who follow him form an irresistible force. What began as a small, vulnerable, persecuted body of women and men is now a strong, healthy, powerful force for good in the world. This is like the parable in the Gospel comparing faith with a grain of seed planted in the ground which subsequently produces a fulsome crop (Mark 4: 28).

The year following the conquest is known as the year of deputations. Many clans sent emissaries to enter peace treaties with Muhammad, including some Christian communities. Hostility against the *ummah*, however, did not cease. Pagan tribes "eager to regain the Ka'bah" gathered to attack the Muslims, mustering a large army of about 4,000 (Ali, 444 n. 1247). In February 630, Muhammad led 12,000 troops against them. They were ambushed by the enemy at Hunayn, almost routed, then recovered, stood their ground and defeated the allies. Fugitives fleeing from their defeat took refuge in the fortress of al-Taif, which then made "preparations for war" (Guillaume, 587). The Battle of Hunayn and the subsequent siege of Taif later the same month are linked with Surah 9. When it became apparent, after 20 days, that Taif would take long to conquer, Muhammad lifted the siege, saying it would be better to win them over than to wage a wasteful campaign. Shortly after this, Muhammad again performed *Umrah*. By December 630, Taif was negotiating a treaty. They wanted, however, to retain their idol. Eventually they agreed; the idol was destroyed and a Muslim governor was appointed to rule over the city. In October 630, hearing that Heraclius, the Byzantine Emperor, intended to attack, Muhammad led an army to Tabuk. Muir says that Muhammad led 30,000 men (1912, 441). The rumour about an attack proved false and by December Muhammad had returned to Medina. In March 631 Abu Bakr led the pilgrimage. Muhammad did not participate. In late 631 and early 632, deputations continued to negotiate alliances.

One deputation of some 60 Christians, led by a bishop, came from Najran. According to Ibn Ishaq, 20 Christians from this area had converted to Islam during the Meccan period (Guillaume, 179). Ibn Ishaq's account of the meeting between Muhammad and the Christians says that some 80 verses of Surah 3 were revealed at this time (Guillaume, 272). When it was time for the Christians to pray, Muhammad "allowed them to pray" in his mosque, "which they did, facing east" (Lings, 324). Surah 5: 48 may also date from this encounter, which ended with a treaty between Muhammad and the Christians (Lings, 322). They would remain Christian, but in return for payment of a special tax (*jizya*) were to depend on the *ummah* to defend and protect them. No monastery or church would be destroyed. They became a *dhimmi*, or protected community, linked with 9: 29. In 632, Muhammad led the pilgrimage known as the Farewell Pilgrimage; Surah 110 was revealed at this time, "which he received as an announcement of approaching death" (Pickthall, xv). On Mount Arafat, he preached his last sermon; knowing he would not meet his people there again, he asked, "Have I faithfully delivered unto you my message?" and they shouted, "O God, yea." Surah 5: 3 was revealed (Lings, 334). Shortly before his death, several rival prophets and one prophetess appeared. The danger was that they might claim leadership of the community after his death. This crisis was quickly averted; all were deposed or eliminated before they could present a real threat.

Muhammad's Death: The Last Revelations

In May 632 Muhammad ordered another expedition against Muta. Very soon after, he fell ill. The poison had slowly worked its way through his system. He is said to have constantly repeated Surah 110. While ill, he appointed Abu Bakr to lead the public prayers. Cared for by his wives, he died in Aisha's arms on 8 June 632. Abu Bakr immediately recited Surah 3: 138, "Apostles have passed away before", so if Muhammad "were to die or be killed" will "you turn back on your heels?" (Guillaume, 683; my rendering). If anyone worshipped Muhammad, said Abu Bakr, he was dead, but for those who worshipped God, God was very much alive (Lings, 342).

Surah 110 is one of the shortest *surahs*. Ali takes it to be the last complete passage to be revealed, which suggests that 5 and 9 are composite. Pickthall says it came a few weeks before Muhammad's death (734). My rendering is:

> Allah has comforted you with a great victory,
> Now multitudes are embracing God's religion,
> So praise God and pray for forgiveness; God always responds graciously
> (*tawwaban*).

The title, "Succour" (*Al-Nasr*), is from *nasru* in verse 1, which I have interpreted as "comfort". Denffer comments that the last revelation came nine days before Muhammad's death (28).

Surah 5 has 120 verses. Called "The Feast", the name is from the reference in verse 112 to Jesus calling down a meal for his disciples. Pickthall places this *surah* somewhere between the fifth and tenth years AH, but accepts that verse 3 is "undoubtedly the latest of the whole Qur'an" probably revealed during Muhammad's Farewell Pilgrimage (100). Lings includes part of 5: 3, "this day I have perfected your religion", in Muhammad's Last Sermon (334). Christian–Muslim relations are a central concern. Verse 69 is very similar to 2: 62 and some apply the same argument on abrogation, except that this is later than 3: 85. Surah 69 is also after 51, which says, "do not take Jews and Christians as friends", and this is before 82, which describes Christians as closest in affection to Muslims. The same verse describes Jews and pagans as at enmity with Muslims. An earlier verse, 5 permits Muslims to marry Jewish and Christian women (following Wadud, we can add men) and to eat their food. Verse 48 says that God revealed for each people of the Book a law (*shira'*) and a way (*minhaj*), so instead of disputing they should compete with each other in all virtue. God will finally judge their difference. Other verses are critical of Christians and Jews; they make false exclusive religious claims, they make lawful what is unlawful, while the former blaspheme by calling God a "Trinity" and committing *shirk*. The latter blaspheme by calling Allah "close-fisted" (Ali, 268 n. 772). Strengthened by the Holy Spirit, Jesus spoke from the cradle and into adulthood only the Truth; never ever did he invite people to worship him or his mother or any other false god (see verse 116). Mary was full of truth. The bird from clay is repeated at verse 110, as are curing lepers, raising the dead and healing the sick. The disciples requested food, so Jesus by God's leave brought down a feast for them from heaven. This has been linked with the feeding of the crowd at John 6, with the miraculous catch of fish at Luke 5 and also with the

Last Supper (Ali, 285 n. 825). The lesson is that having asked for a sign which they received, the disciples were doubly obligated to remain on the true path of Unitarian faith. They failed the test, breaking their covenant.

Yet at about the same time, Muhammad was allowing Christians to pray in his mosque, guaranteeing them safety and protection. Esack's view that those Christians or Jews whom Muslims should not befriend were wrongdoers leaves open the possibility that some, on the "right path" can become *wilayah*. Your true friends are those who pray and give to charity (Esack 1997, 181). Jealousy and arrogance can lead, sometimes, to murder; here we have the only reference to Adam's two sons. Ali sees this as a veiled allusion to the wrong type of rivalry between different faiths, rather than the virtuous competition described at 5: 48. Cain (who is not specifically named) repented when God sent a raven who showed him how to hide Abel's corpse, and this brought home to him the enormity of his crime (Ali, 255). Had God willed, God could have destroyed Jesus, his mother and all humanity to pre-empt blasphemy. Christians and Jews claim to be children of Allah but fail to please God, or at least some fail. Those who wage war against Muhammad are liable to severe punishment, says verse 33, crucifixion, amputation or exile.

True believers, as described at verse 8, are those who deal fairly, uphold justice, fear God and do not let hatred of others distract them from doing what is right. This definition does not obviously exclude Christians and Jews, and others who stand in pragmatic solidarity with the *mustad'afun* (oppressed) of the earth. Esack argues that the injunction against taking Others as friends does not apply to Others who either are among the oppressed or stand in solidarity with Muslims in combating oppression (1997, 193). The term "downtrodden" or "dispossessed" is used, for example, at 4: 97 when angels ask us at Judgement Day if we were of the oppressed, and at 8: 25–6 and 28: 5. Opening verses deal with the *hajj*, mentioning the pilgrim's garb, and encourage mutual help and solidarity. The wicked must not be aided. Verses also reiterate dietary rules and ritual ablution before prayer. The words "this day I have completed my favour, I have perfected your religion and given you Islam as the true path", perhaps the very last revelation, would have comforted Muhammad in his illness. His work was finished. Part of this verse, "if hunger compels you to transgress", carries forward to verse 39, which prescribes amputation as the *hud* (limit) penalty for theft. If anyone who is not lazy but genuinely cannot find work is forced to steal to feed their family, the whole community is guilty. Distributed efficiently, *Zakat* should provide a safety net. However, a repentant thief should be given clemency. What is evil can never be equivalent to what is good. Verses 90–1 repeat the prohibition against gambling, sorcery and use of intoxicants, worded more strongly than at 2: 219; Satan lures us with such abominations. The *haram–halal*, permitted–prohibited, distinction is briefly discussed in my Conclusion, as is the concept of *hudud*. Some Muslims regard amputation as the only correct punishment for theft, although limitations were set relating to the value of the stolen object, which had to exceed a set minimum (3 *dirhams* during Muhammad's life, Bukhari, 81: 787). Others argue that what is eternal and immutable is the ethical principle, or ideal, the norm behind the particular application as described in the Qur'an, not the penalty itself. This verse was actually revealed in connection with the theft of "a piece of armor" (Denffer, 100). The Qur'an, we are reminded, is a clear message. It confirms and corrects previous scriptures. Muslims should obey Muhammad (verse 92).

Surah 9, the only *surah* without the *bismillah*, has 129 verses. The title, "*tawbah*" means "Repentance". It is, though, the same word used above at 110: 3 which I interpreted as "responds graciously" and at for example 2: 37, which says that God "relented" towards Adam. There, *attawwabu* is followed by *alrraheemu* (Merciful). God as repenting does not work theologically, so forgiving, turning towards or being gracious may be better. God is "oft-returning", says Ali (26). Speculation differs on why *bismillahi* is lacking. Some scholars suggest it was left incomplete, interrupted by Muhammad's death. This, though, does not explain why the *bismillah* would not have been inserted at the beginning, since this indicated when a new passage was starting. Ali says there is no evidence that Muhammad prefixed the *bismillah* and that the passage was possibly intended to form part of Surah 8 (435). Pickthall suggests that absence of the *bismillah* reflects the stern content (178). However, many regard it as the final, or penultimate, *surah*. Described in the tradition as a sword verse, 9: 5 may be the most widely cited passage of all. I have read books on religion and conflict in which this is the only verse from the Qur'an. Content follows closely on that of Surah 5. The dominant concern is for the light of truth to banish falsehood. Muslims protect each other, repel evil, give to the poor and pray. Here, 9: 71 refers explicitly to women and men as protectors of each other; there is no hint that women are subordinate to men. Muslims are to strive to defeat evil and end idolatry, to God's glory. Throughout the *surah*, some are rebuked for their reluctance to strive or fight when necessary. Some fear that a *surah* will descend that reveals what is really in their hearts. The Ansaris are praised for helping the Muhajirs. They are the Vanguard of Islam. Polytheists do not even acknowledge as family any believer who is related to them, despite the sanctity of blood ties. Several have context-specific content. For example, 9: 25 refers to God's help at Hunayn, when the Muslims were almost routed. With the odds in their favour, they were prone to be self-reliant, not reliant on God. Those not recruited to march to Tabuk were only too happy to stay behind (9: 81). Verse 40 refers to Muhammad and Abu Bakr in the Cave during the *hijrah*. Verse 107 refers to one of the rival mosques, "put up by mischief". Some desert Arabs and others had a variety of excuses not to fight; some thought their wealth exempted them (verses 85, 93). Some wanted to stay with their women. Some even regard their *zakat* as a fine, which they resent having to pay. *Zakat*, says verse 60, is reserved exclusively for the poor. Only the blind and sick and disabled have a legitimate reason for exemption. Some, though, should remain behind in reserve. Picking up on 60: 4, verses 113–14 say that Muslims should not pray for a pagan, unlike Abraham in his tender-hearted compassion, even for a kin. People are responsible for their own eternal destiny. Christians are criticized at verse 31 for investing too much authority in their leaders, taking Jesus and even their "lords" as gods. Their leaders also take more than they are entitled from their flocks. Verse 30 says that Jews too wrongly use the term "sons of God" (see Job 38: 7; Genesis 6: 2).

Verses 20 and 41 use the word "strive" (*wajahidu*) in a way that can be interpreted to refer to what the tradition calls *jihad bis saif*, *jihad* of the sword; Muslims are encouraged to strive with their wealth and their lives in God's cause. If slain, paradise awaits them. Controversy surrounding this *surah* centres on verses 1, 5 and 29. Ordinarily, the Qur'an uses *qital* or *harb* for "fight". Verse 1 has been interpreted to mean that Muslims are no longer to enter any treaties with pagans; Ibn Kathir, citing an earlier exegete, says, "No idolater had any more treaty or promise of treaty" since this *surah* was revealed. However, existing treaties remained valid until they expired, all of which had fixed terms (Ibn Kathir, vol. 4, pp. 375–7). Others took the view that while new, temporary treaties could be negotiated, a perpetual war exists between the House of Islam and the non-Muslim world until the former absorbs the latter, by persuasion or by conquest. Al-Ghazali, cited in Chapter 3, condemned the view that this verse permits unlimited aggression. He and others argue that the context remains an ongoing war. "When the sacred months have ended, slay the pagans wherever you find them", using "every strategy", not merely waiting for them to come to you, describes the resumption of hostility after the four-month armistice has ended. Verse 36 says that God divided the year into 12 months at creation, and declared four to be sacred. Treaties, unless broken, are to be honoured; if pagans respect and keep the Treaty, these "are not dissolved" (verse 4). Fight those who violate their oaths, says verse 13; God will give you victory. Muslims are to keep their oaths (see 16: 91). The ban at verse 28 on pagans visiting the Ka'bah points to a post-630 date. The reference at verse 29 to fighting the People of the Book until they agree to pay the *jizya* and are humbled became the basis of the *dhimma* arrangement. Some Muslims interpreted this to mean that, when paying the tax, *dhimmi* should be humiliated. They should grovel and be struck on the head. Others cite the oft-repeated *hadith*, "he who harms a *dhimmi*, harms me" and suggest that "humility" here refers to pragmatic recognition, in their particular circumstances, of Islam's superior political and military status. Umar urged his successor to take care of *dhimmis*, not to tax them beyond their capacity (Bukhari, 52: 287). Far from the Qur'an "casting Christianity contemptuously aside" as Muir says with "abasement and cruel words" (454), it leaves open a real possibility of genuine dialogue and common action to eliminate poverty, and to establish peace and global justice for all people. Islam is the *Dar-al-Salaam*, Home of Peace; it cannot be the motive for unprovoked aggression or for acts of terror (10: 25). The Qur'an repeatedly demands *adl*, justice; the use of Surah 9: 5 to justify killing non-combatants subverts this. The oldest rules of engagement, written by Abu Bakr, protect crops, animals, priests, women, children, the sick and the elderly (see Sultan 2007, 166). Even in self-defence, response must be proportionate to the acts of aggression or oppression that provoke this; Allah, who prefers self-restraint, limits the use of force (2: 190; 2: 194).

Analysis

When Muhammad died, the whole of Arabia was under Islamic governance. Soon, the green standard would fly over an even larger territory. Shortly after Muhammad's death, the Ansari convened a *shura* to choose a leader for the community. The *muhajirs* were not present, so this was an attempt to pre-empt the leadership. Informed about the gathering, Abu Bakr and Umar hastened to the meeting. The former was unanimously selected as Caliph. If I govern, he said, according to my own opinion, impeach me, but if I govern according to Qur'an and *sunnah*, follow me. He would strengthen the weak and end oppression (Muir, 502). No one could, the majority believed, succeed him as prophet or claim inspiration, but the *ummah* needed a Deputy (Caliph) to lead politically, a military commander (*Amir*) and an *Imam* to stand first in prayer, symbolizing the unity of the whole community. Caliphs should rule according to the Qur'an and *sunnah*, however, consulting others in the process. Of course, theory has not always translated into practice, which the Conclusion will discuss. A minority party, the Shi'a later argued that male descendants of Muhammad, beginning with Ali, continued to be inspired. Only they, said the Shi'a, could lead the community as Imam.

Some argue that Muhammad died without finalizing a system for governing the *ummah*. This was not, actually, his prerogative. The system for governance was set out in the Qur'an itself, with *shura* as the mechanism for succeeding generations to devise a government to meet the needs of their day. If Muhammad's motive had been gaining worldly, kingly power he would have requested his followers to pledge *bayat* (allegiance) to his heirs, as they did to Abu Bakr after his selection, or even election. Rather, he was God's prophet, who humbly signed all documents "Allah's Apostle". He died leaving little property. He took nothing from the treasury for himself. His last words, reported by Aisha, were, "Muhammad is of the blessed Company of those who live righteously, of those upon whom God has gifted grace, the beautiful fellowship of all the prophets who teach truth, who offer sincere witness" (4: 69; my rendering) (Lings, 341). The Conclusion outlines the role of the Qur'an in Muslim life, then discusses several exegetical issues raised in the last four chapters.

Conclusion: The Qur'an in Muslim Life and Practice with Final Thoughts

This concluding chapter begins with the role of the Qur'an in Muslim faith, life and practice. Next it touches on the legal significance of the Qur'an, which becomes a bridge into discussion of several exegetical issues raised in previous chapters. We visit Qur'anic penalties, war and peace, gender, previous scriptures, science and the Qur'an, the uncreated, eternal nature of the Qur'an, verses of "likening" and of "incomparability", and end with a final reflection.

Calligraphy: Khatt

"For Muslims", says Esack, "the Qur'an is alive and has a quasi-human personality" (2005, 17). Effectively, Muslims regard the Qur'an as an extension of the divine into human space. As such, presence of the Qur'an in Muslim life is ubiquitous. As Muslims go about their lives, they are constantly reminded of verses that relate to the task or job in hand. Surah *fatiha* which opens each *rakhat* (cycle) of prayer is recited at least 17 times a day. Popularly, amulets contain appropriate verses to guard against sickness or to ward off evil. Surah 2: 155, the "Throne Verse" may be pasted behind doors (Esack, 18). Noah's prayer at 11: 41 is stuck "on the windscreens of vehicles from Chicago to Jakarta". While the Qur'an does not explicitly ban representational art, that is, depictions of the human form, Islam discourages this.

Although representational art does exist within the Muslim world, the major art form is calligraphy, or beautiful handwriting. Calligraphy overlaps with representation by forming shapes of birds, plants and fruits. The Arabic term, *Khatt*, denotes "line". It gives us the term *husn-al-khatt*, beautiful writing. God, says the Qur'an, loves beauty (*hassana*) at such verses as 2: 83 and 5: 13, and at 33: 21 it refers to Muhammad's *sunnah*, which can be rendered as "beautiful" or "noble". A *hadith* says, "Allah is beautiful and

11th century North African Qur'an, British Museum. Public Domain. (Image 1)

loves beauty" (Leaman, 311). Muhammad said, "Beauty of handwriting is incumbent upon you, for it is one of the keys of man's daily bread." Tradition has it that God taught Adam use of the pen (see 96: 4). "Handwriting", said al-Tawhidi (d. 1023) is "jewelry fashioned by the hand from the pure gold of the intellect" (Nasr, 17).

Calligraphy produces beautiful copies of the sacred text, which Muslims only touch after washing their hands. Esack mentions friends who do not change clothes in their bedrooms because they keep a copy of the Qur'an there (2005, 17). In addition, calligraphy carries relevant and appropriate verses into everyday life. Objects such as plates, bowels, utensils, pens and ink-pots are inscribed with words from the Qur'an. Often, because of limited space, a short phrase symbolizes the whole passage. Calligraphy is inscribed on the exterior and interiors of public and private buildings. Whole walls and surfaces may be covered; a famous example is the verses on the blue-tiled circumference of the Dome of the

bismillahi (fruit hanging from branch) (Image 2)

Rock in Jerusalem, which includes every Qur'anic verse about Jesus. The whole Al-Aqsa area contains over 4,000 Qur'anic inscriptions. A popular passage is Surah 48, which is often cited in full. The Taj Mahal complex has numerous examples of calligraphy, including *Fath*. Graves have inscriptions describing paradise. Framed calligraphy, such as the *bismillahi*, is found in office and home alike.

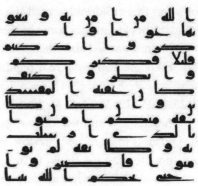

7th century Q7: 86–7, Kufic script, National Library, St. Petersburg, Russia. Public Domain (Image 3).

Calligraphers are highly skilled. Over time, different styles developed. The square, thicker, angular Kufic script was one of the earliest forms, associated with Kufa in Iraq.

The most common form is the thinner cursive *Naskh* script (from "copy"; the same word as for the theory of abrogation), which is widely used in printing as well as for handwriting, usually taught to children. The *bismillahi* in *Naskh* look like this:

بسم الله الر حمن الر حيم

Islamic calligraphy is related to geometry; symmetry, harmony, pattern and use of space, such as extending a letter above to stretch across the page, are essential features. Rules governing the art-form were written at an early stage. It has been said that "decoration" in Islam, which also makes much use of geometric patterns and mosaic, is actually not "decorative" or "cosmetic" in a trivial sense but reflects the very order of the cosmos. Calligraphy, mosaic, pattern, stretch from the divine into places of human habitation. Traditionally, a reed pen and Indian ink were preferred. Before beginning their work, calligraphers perform a *rakhat* of prayer. One convention is to leave a slight flaw in the work; only God is perfect, the supreme artist (2: 138).

Tajwid

Attending Qur'an school, learning to recite some passages or the whole Book, is an important part of children's religious nurture and formation. This does not mean that children learn all the rules of the science or art of recitation, although they do master some of these. Rules relate to when to pause, when to lengthen the vowel and when to assimilate the sound of one letter with the next. There are also *ayahs* that require a "prostration when you read or hear them", namely 7: 206; 13: 15; 16: 49–50; 17: 109; 19: 58; 22: 18; 22: 77; 25: 60; 27: 25, 26; 32:15, 38:24–5; 41: 38; 53: 62; 84: 20–1 and 96: 19 (Denffer, 166). It is permitted or recommended to stop at certain points, compulsory at others. The Qur'an is to be recited "in slow, rhythmic tones" (73: 4). Night is a auspicious time to read the Book, facing the *qiblah*. There are different modes of recitation as well as what are known as the seven *ahruf*, or "readings" and other schools of recitation. Differences are minor; they relate to how some words and sentences are pronounced. Recitation, however, is for hearing not "writing about"; explore http://quranexplorer.com/. Sells' book comes with a CD, *The Call to Prayer and Six Surahs*.

The Qur'an and Law in Islamic Contexts

For millions of Muslims, the Qur'an is the source of spiritual wisdom, an aid to developing *taqwa* (consciousness) of God as omnipresent in their lives. Like God, the Qur'an is also omnipresent, so whether Muslims are at work, worship or play they remain aware that God expects them to obey his "law". *Dhikr*, remembrance of God's Names, derived from the Qur'an, is one of the most widely practised devotional acts. The Qur'an is "full of *dhikr*" (38: 1). *Dhikr* is especially, although not exclusively, associated with the Sufi, or mystical tendency in Islam. Sufi Muslims, who stress the inner meaning of the Qur'an, have sometimes found themselves in tension with the more legalistic tradition. The Qur'an, however, does serve a legal or ethical function within Muslim life on a day-to-day basis; it relates to how Muslims greet people when they pass them in the street; to what they do and do not eat; and to how they observe the five *fard* (mandatory) religious duties. A great deal of *adab* (behaviour) is directly or indirectly Qur'anic. In addition to acts and substances that the Qur'an prohibits, other behaviour and foods are clearly disapproved of (*makruh*), such as slander (Surah 60: 12).

While Muhammad was alive, his position as head of the *ummah* was a given. As the inspired prophet, his rulings and his example complemented the Qur'an. For example, he disliked music, so many Muslims consider music *makruh*. He did not shave, so many Muslims consider this *makruh*, although for some both music and shaving are *haram*. Sitting on your heels at prayer, smoking tobacco and eating donkey-meat are *makruh*. Technically, *haram* acts can attract punishment, so these issues are not trivial. If the Qur'an is interpreted as prescribing *hijab* for women, for example, this has implications in a Muslim society that decides to legally enforce dress codes. After Muhammad's death, the early caliphs said that they would rule according to the Qur'an and *hadith*. Such matters as inheritance, marriage, divorce and aspects of criminal law, including murder, adultery, fornication and theft, are dealt with in the Qur'an, so such passages, with appropriate material from the *hadith*, became the foundation of *shari'ah*, or law (from "a path that leads to a watering hole"). Examples of *hadith* complementing the Qur'an are the banishment of Christians and Jews from the Hijaz due to a saying that "two religions can not exist in Arabia" (Hughes, 57), and the penalty of stoning for a married partner guilty of adultery with an unmarried man or woman (Bukhari, 82: 804–10).

Yet sometimes it was necessary to "apply" the Qur'an to a novel situation. Many Muslims believe that the Qur'an contains all knowledge, even scientific knowledge, so the issue was not one of extending the Qur'an (which only the *hadith* can do) but of applying Qur'anic principles (*usul*) to new contexts. This led to the science of jurisprudence (*fiqh*). It is inappropriate here to describe *fiqh* methods or the development of *shari'ah* in great detail; however, aspects of *fiqh* create a bridge into the next segment of this Conclusion, which returns to several exegetical issues. The main tool that the *fuqaha* (jurists) used was *ijma*, consensus; what the learned took to be the authentic Islamic position became exactly that. An individual scholar of renown might employ *ijtihad* (personal effort) to deduce a position, from rigorous study of Qur'an and *hadith*, but this still had to attract a consensus. In the reasoning process, such devices as *qiyas* (analogy) and *masalah* (concern for public welfare) played crucial roles. Local custom (*urf*) was allowed, too, if this did not contradict the Qur'an, or what might be called the 'spirit' of the Qur'an. The caliphate itself rested on *ijma*. Four main, recognized Sunni schools emerged, with, it is said, minor differences and no major disagreements. The same formula is used with respect of the *ahruf*.

At least in theory, the caliphs were subject to the *shari'ah*, not above the law. The Shi'a took a different approach, believing that Muhammad's male heirs possessed a special ability to interpret the Qur'an, inheriting his *nur* (light) (see Surah 33: 46). However, none of the 12 Imams recognized by the majority of Shi'a exercised actual political authority, because during their lifetimes the Shi'a existed as an underground minority. When Iran became a Shi'a state, the Imam was no longer "present" but Hidden in heaven. Wishing to avoid discussing difference between Sunni (followers of the Sunnah) and Shi'a jurisprudence, I focus in what follows on the former. By the eleventh century, the power of the Abbasid caliphs was in decline. Real authority was delegated to Sultans, who ruled what were technically provinces, later autonomous states. Claiming that their duty was to protect *sharia'h*, the rulers found ways of bypassing this in favour of their own edicts, or administrative orders. This resulted in many areas of the law departing from Islamic norms.

Much later, when almost the entire Muslim world became subject to colonial rule, *shari'ah* was reduced in scope even further. Following decolonization, Muslim countries around the world found that what was in place as legal systems and governance was based on European models. Throughout the Muslim world, the call has been to revive Islamic patterns and models and to restore full-blown *shari'ah*. For some Muslims, this includes amputation for theft, stoning for adultery and dress-codes enforceable by law. Based on their understanding of Surah 4: 35 as reading "men are in charge of women", some Muslim men want to legally restrict women's employment to exclude, for example, serving as head of state or of government. When Benazir Bhutto became Prime Minister of Pakistan in 1988, many men denounced this as a violation of *shari'ah*, citing a *hadith*, "those who entrust their affairs to a woman will never know prosperity" (Mernissi, 49). Linked to gender equality are inheritance issues and testimonial issues: Is it mandatory in a Muslim system that two women must give evidence while one man's testimony can suffice? Must a Muslim society retain the death penalty because this is prescribed as the maximum punishment for homicide? Must a Muslim society retain and sometimes use amputation for theft as the maximum penalty available in law? Or, are such penalties incompatible with modern notions of humane punishment and with universal human rights? If so, how can the Qur'an be the final, complete, definitive expression of God's will for humanity?

Rethinking the Qur'an

Some Muslims answer "Yes" to questions about the absolute sanctity of Qur'anic penalties remaining available under any authentic Islamic justice and legal system. Others argue that the *ethical voice* of the Qur'an takes priority over *legal content*. Such Muslims argue that while the message of the Qur'an is universal, it was revealed within a particular historical, social and cultural context. The eternal message, they argue, is to be found in the *intent and spirit*, not in the *content* of legal and ethical passages. For example, the Qur'an does not prohibit slavery but encourages manumission so strongly that logic compels us to abolish this as the rational response (see Bukhari, Book 46 on the merits of manumission). Some Muslims argue that the whole notion of an Islamic state is based on a misunderstanding of history. Muhammad, they say, became a political ruler from necessity, but Muslims are free to separate "religion" and "state" if they choose. Many more Muslims, though, believe that Islam should shape governance; many want *shari'ah* to be the law of the land. In contexts where Muslims are a majority, it is for them to decide by *shura* (42: 38) how to organize religion–state relations. At issue, though, is how Muslims interpret *shari'ah*. On the one hand, traditional interpretations are available; these retain gender inequality, capital and corporal punishment. On the other hand, a range of alternative interpretations are also possible. Progressive Muslims suggest that by applying the intent of the Qur'an, which set *hud* punishments as the limit while always encouraging clemency, these can be substituted for punishments that today's society considers appropriate and humane. A long, maximum jail sentence, for example, can substitute for amputation. God dealt with people in the seventh century as God found them; it is the *principles* not the *applications* that God wants us to enshrine in our legal systems today.

Some Muslims, such as M. M. Taha (1909–85) went further, arguing that the general, universal ethical principles of the Meccan verses, which contain no specific penalties and not the slightest hint at gender inequality, represent the "original" message. These cancel, or abrogate, the later "subsidiary" Medinan passages. People were not prepared for the full ethical intent of the Qur'an, so God responded with what, effectively, was a "descent" from Islam's real message and meaning (Taha, 161). *Jihad* (understood as unprovoked aggression), slavery, polygamy or the veil, he said, were not "original precepts in Islam" (137–43). *Jihad* as self-defence or as a just war may be consistent with the Qur'an's ethical intent, although some Muslims regard Muhammad's pacifist stance at Mecca as the ideal; he was to change hearts with gentle persuasion, diplomacy and dialogue (16: 125). Even if war with Mecca was a pragmatic necessity condoned by God, this does not mean that God condones war today. Incidentally, the abrogation argument on war as on other issues has had universal support. Every "passage or practice that is held abrogated by one scholar", says Esack, "is questioned by another" (2005, 127). On war and peace, Esack argues that the balance of Qur'anic verses favour peace, but that other verses do permit, justify and even "encourage armed struggle in defence of one's freedom and rights" (2005, 190). Ibn Kathir identified 22: 39 as the first "verse of jihad", meaning *jihad* of the sword. Muslims have used *jihad* to refer both to defensive wars and to aggressive territorial expansion. Yet almost all Qur'anic occurrences of *jhd* exhort spiritual striving or the struggle to establish justice; when the Qur'an explicitly discusses fighting it uses a different word. To render *jihad* as "Holy War" is incorrect. A popular saying calls armed *jihad* the "lesser *jihad*"; the greater *jihad* is peaceful (the saying is not found in the classical collection).

Gender Issues

Writers such as Leila Ahmed and Fatimah Mernissi argue that the *ethical intent* of the Qur'an calls for *complete equality*. This is indicated by a Meccan verse such 16: 72 but also by 33: 35, from Medina. Muslim men were unprepared to concede complete gender equality, so verses on inheritance, evidence and other gender-related issues such as different divorce procedures were revealed as concessions. However, the universal ethical spirit takes priority. The way in which verses, too, have been interpreted by men has served men's interests. There is no need to translate *daraba* as "beat" or "*Ma Malakat Aymanukum*" – "those whom your right hand possesses" – as "concubines", but men have chosen to do so. In her detailed examination of mysogynist *hadith*, such as Muhammad seeing more women than men in hell (Bukhari, 76: 456) and the saying about not trusting governance to a woman, Mernissi found that many did not pass scrutiny. Either the narrator's reputation was suspect or Aisha, in the collection edited by Zarkash, contradicted their version. It was the narrators, she concluded, not Muhammad, who had a problem with women! The saying about women leaders was conveniently "remembered" after the failure of the Aisha-led rebellion against Ali at the Battle of the Camel in 656 to justify the narrator's own failure to support the revolt (Mernissi, 50–1). Umar had punished him for lying. A more intimate companion of Muhammad than this narrator, Umar was reluctant to cite *hadith*, lest he make a false attribution to the prophet (Mernissi, 70). Yet this suspect *hadith* is "omnipresent and all embracing" in any debate about women's involvement in politics (4).

Wadud points out that the Qur'an offers no criticism of the Queen of Sheba for governing her nation, which, if this was an issue, we might expect; beyond identifying "her as a woman, no distinction, restriction, limitation, or speci-fication of her as a woman is ever mentioned" (Wadud, 40). Ahmed argues that as the caliphate expanded into an empire, with more and more women captured in battle, which made concubines easily available, the distinction between "women" and "object" as in "sexual object" blurred (Ahmed, 85). Consequently, women were divided into elite women on the one hand and sex-objects on the other: the former were secluded and veiled; the latter were looked on as inferior and immoral, although the men who used them appar-ently remained pure. Yet "a reading by a less androcentric and less misogynist society, one that gave greater ear to the ethical voice of the Qur'an, could have resulted in – could someday result in – the elaboration of laws that dealt equitably with women", says Ahmed (91). Muhammad's multiple marriages have attracted censure from non-Muslims. Muslims point out that many of his marriages either established important political alliances or took care of widows, the exact intent of Surah 4: 3. While non-Muslims may still choose to regard the verse that allegedly permitted Muhammad to exceed four wives as self-indulgent fabrication, it has to be said that Muslims simply do not regard Muhammad's marriages as problematic. Rather, they look to Muhammad as an example of how to manage domestic life. Since Jesus did not marry, they say, he has little to offer Christians by way of guidance in this area. Others point out that God has allowed prophets a degree of licence; Solomon had 700 wives and 300 concubines (1 Kings 11: 3).

Tahrif: Is the Bible Corrupt?

We identified some verses that question the validity of previous scriptures. On the one hand, Muslims are required to *believe in these scriptures*. On the other hand, there is some doubt about their accuracy. In contrast, there is no doubt about the Qur'an, so most Muslims take the view that there is little point reading earlier scriptures if they are probably corrupt. Some Muslims argue, though, that the verses on *tahrif* do not necessarily assert textual corruption; they can be understood to refer to verbal misinterpretation, to a twisting of the words, a concealment of the truth (see 2: 75; 4: 46; 5: 13; 5: 41). The *Injil* mentioned in the Qur'an, though, would not correspond with the four Gospels, which are more similar to *sirah* than to they are to the Qur'an. Jesus would not have claimed to be God's Son. Yet if the Bible had no validity, why would Muhammad have been told to consult the People of the Book when in any doubt about the meaning of a Revelation (2: 121)? Esack, who does not accept that the Verses of Hostility (such as 5: 51) cancel the Verses of Friendship (such as 2: 62), asks why marriage with Christian and Jewish women and eating their food would be permitted if friendship was prohibited (Esack 1997, 160). It is with those who mock Islam (5: 57) that friendship becomes impossible.

Issues surrounding Jesus' crucifixion remain on the table for Christian–Muslim dialogue. So, too, does the incarnation, God becoming flesh. The Qur'an says that God has no "son". On a theological level, Christian belief in the eternal, uncreated Word of God becoming flesh is similar to Muslim belief in the eternal, uncreated Word becoming a book. Both represent the *uncreated* entering the *created* world. In the incarnation, God takes on human form. In the sending down of the Word in Islam, the Word becomes a Book, which consists of ink and paper. One Christian reply to Islam could be that a God who can say "Be" to create the world could also say "Be", and allow a "part" of God's-self to be born as a man. Christians do not believe that the whole of God became human; part of God did so. Each person of the Trinity, individually, is *wholly God* (*Totus Dei*) but not the *whole of God* (*Totum Dei*). This resonates with some of the ways in which certain aspects of the message of the Qur'an have been understood.

An Eternal Qur'an

As *Kalam*, God's Word, the Qur'an is regarded as eternal. God's Word, like God's power, mercy or justice, always existed. The Qur'an may, at a point in time, have been transcribed onto the Heavenly Tablet, but as Word, it pre-existed from eternity within the Godness of God, just as Jesus in Christian thought is eternally begotten. Members of a school known as Mutazalites were unhappy with this; to them, it compromised God's unity. If God and God's Book existed side by side, did Muslims worship two Gods? Was this not *shirk*? The Mutazalites argued for an uncreated Qur'an, citing, "we have *made* it an Arabic Qur'an" (43: 3) For a while, the Mutazalites enjoyed the support of the Abbasid caliphs, who thought that a created Qur'an enhanced their own authority. If the Qur'an was not eternal, their rulings could take priority, since the Qur'an might be contingent on the contexts in which it was revealed. From 813 to 847, only people who signed a Mutazalite creed could hold office. Their critics, who became known as Asharites after the great theologian al-Ashari (d. 936), defended the uncreated Qur'an. However, God's eternal Word is not to be confused with the paper and ink of a *mushaf*, he said. These are man-made and created. When the written, bookified word is pronounced, what we hear is nothing less than the very speech of God. The Asharite view dominated. The Mutazalites also rejected the emerging view that God's many attributes or qualities (*sifat*), which permeate the Qur'an, are co-eternal and co-equal with God, existing within God's nature. If there was never a single moment when God did not embody justice, then this quality, like God's Word, must have existed from eternity. However, God's justness (*Adl*) is distinct from God's power (*al-Qudrah*), while both are distinct from God's Word. All these qualities, at least 99 of them, are on the one hand *wholly God* while on the other hand they are not *the whole of God*; each is also distinct, God's Word is distinct from God's power, God's power from God's mercy.

Science in the Qur'an

Much has been written about the compatibility of thr Qur'an with science. Muslims find all types of knowledge in the Qur'an, ranging from management theory to algebra. Many claims are made that it anticipates or predicts discoveries and advances in modern scientific thought. Muslims point out many interesting facts: the statement about seven heavens occurs seven times; the singular "day" occurs 365 times; month occurs 12 times; Satan and angels balance equally at 88, as do "paradise" and "hell" at 77. For Muslims, all this confirms the inimitable and incomparable (*'ijaz*) nature of the Qur'an, suggesting that no piecemeal process of human composition over time could possibly have achieved such perfection. A browse on the web will uncover much material here.

Verses of Likening and Verses that Prohibit Comparison

Debate about the verses of "likening" (*tasbih*) and of "incomparability" (*tanzih*) relates to thinking about *sifat*. We encountered verses implying that God has a throne, such as 57: 4. If so, does God sit on this throne? Verses such as 17: 1 and 42: 11 speak of God as seeing and hearing. How does he see and hear? Does he have eyes and ears, as we do? If we see God at Judgement Day, implied by 75: 22–3, does God possess a body? Surah 42: 11, as does 112: 4, also says that nothing can be compared with God. Surah 6: 103 says that "vision" can not "grasp God". How, then, are these anthropomorphic verses to be understood? A minority simply accepted the notion that God possessed a body, with eyes and ears. Some argued that verses prohibiting comparison outweighed and therefore cancelled verses of likening; God does not have a body or sensory organs as we do. Nor does God sit on a throne. Others drew on *qiyas*, analogy, to argue their case. The prohibition of the Qur'an on drinking *khamr* (date wine, 2: 219; 5: 90) had been interpreted to ban all intoxicants. Although various intoxicants are made from different substances, have different colour and taste, they share at least one similarity; they make us drunk. So, God does see and hear, but our seeing and hearing and God's are different. On the other hand, if there was no similarity, we would be incapable of saying anything about God. The prohibition on comparing God with anything, then, is to be understood as forbidding comparison in some but not in all respects. Al-Ashari is famous for his formula, "without asking how and without forming comparison" (*bila kayfa wala tasbih*), we accept that God hears and sees "without asking how" (Glassé, 99). Hearing (*as-Sam*) and Sight (*al-Basar*) are among the *sifat*. This can be applied to the booki-fication process in Islam and to incarnation in Christianity; if God is God, omnipotent, unlimited by human ability to comprehend, we can accept that God's Word became a Book and a Person "without asking how".

And Finally

Much, indeed most, of what the Qur'an says is clear and easy to understand; it teaches us that God is merciful and loves those who exercise mercy. God loves those who love the marginalized, who store up treasure in heaven, who give generously and strive against all oppression and injustice. Where we err is when we substitute our understanding for scripture itself, forgetting that while the Qur'an is divine our comprehension is human. Even the greatest *fuqaha*, whose jurisprudence was regarded as nearly perfect, were humble about their interpretations, adding *Allahu a'lam* (God knows better) to their writing. As Esack ends, so do I, "no, not 'best', better – eternally better than anything and everyone" (Esack 2005, 192).

Appendix 1
Comparison of Four Sequences of Revelation

Meccan in Bold	Ibn Abbas	Zarkashi	Nöldeke	Rodwell
1	96	96	96	96
2	68	68	74	74
3	93	73	111	73
4	73	74	106	93
5	74	111	108	94
6	1	81	104	113
7	111	87	107	114
8	81	92	102	1
9	87	89	105	109
10	92	93	92	112
11	89	94	90	111
12	94	103	94	108
13	55	100	13	104
14	103	108	14	107
15	108	102	15	102
16	102	107	16	92
17	107	109	80	68
18	105	105	68	90
19	109	113	87	105
20	112	114	95	106
21	53	112	103	97
22	80	53	85	86
23	97	80	73	91
24	91	97	101	80
25	85	91	99	87
26	95	85	82	95
27	106	95	81	103

Meccan in Bold	Ibn Abbas	Zarkashi	Nöldeke	Rodwell
28	101	106	53	85
29	75	101	84	101
30	104	75	100	99
31	77	104	79	82
32	50	77	77	81
33	90	50	78	84
34	86	90	88	100
35	54	86	89	79
36	38	54	75	77
37	7	38	83	78
38	72	7	69	88
39	36	72	51	89
40	25	36	52	75
41	35	25	56	83
42	19	35	70	69
43	20	19	55	51
44	26	20	112	52
45	27	56	109	56
46	28	26	113	53
47	17	27	114	70
48	10	28	109	55
49	11	17	54	54
50	12	10	37	37
51	15	11	71	71
52	6	12	76	76
53	37	15	44	44
54	31	6	50	50
55	34	37	20	20
56	39	31	26	26
57	40	34	15	15
58	41	39	19	19
59	42	40	38	38
60	43	41	36	36
61	44	42	43	43
62	45	43	72	72
63	46	44	67	67

Meccan in Bold	Ibn Abbas	Zarkashi	Nöldeke	Rodwell
64	**51**	**45**	**23**	**23**
65	**88**	**46**	**21**	**21**
66	**18**	**51**	**25**	**25**
67	**16**	**88**	**17**	**17**
68	**71**	**18**	**27**	**27**
69	**14**	**16**	**18**	**18**
70	**21**	**71**	**32**	**32**
71	**23**	**14**	**41**	**41**
72	**13**	**21**	**45**	**45**
73	**52**	**23**	**16**	**16**
74	**67**	**32**	**30**	**30**
75	**69**	**52**	**11**	**11**
76	**70**	**67**	**14**	**14**
77	**78**	**69**	**12**	**12**
78	**79**	**70**	**40**	**40**
79	**82**	**78**	**28**	**28**
80	**84**	**79**	**39**	**39**
81	**30**	**82**	**29**	**29**
82	**29**	**84**	**31**	**31**
83	**83**	**30**	**42**	**42**
84	**2**	**83**	**10**	**10**
85	**8**	**29**	**34**	**34**
86	3	2	35	35
87	59	8	7	7
88	33	3	46	46
89	24	33	6	6
90	60	60	13	13
91	48	4	2	2
92	4	99	98	98
93	99	57	64	64
94	22	47	94	62
95	57	13	8	8
96	47	55	47	47
97	76	76	3	3
98	65	65	61	61
99	98	98	57	57

Meccan in Bold	Ibn Abbas	Zarkashi	Nöldeke	Rodwell
100	62	59	4	4
101	32	110	65	65
102	63	24	59	59
103	58	22	33	33
104	49	63	63	63
105	66	58	24	24
106	64	49	58	58
107	61	66	22	22
108	5	61	48	48
109	9	62	66	66
110	110	64	60	60
111	56	48	110	110
112	100	9	49	49
113	113	5	46	9
114	114	(1)	47	5

Source for Zarkash, Denffer pages 86–87; for Ibn Abbas, Nöldeke and Rodwell, Fischer and Abedi pages 445–447.

Appendix 2
Verses Revealed at Medina in Meccan Passages and at Mecca in Medinan Passages

1	**31:** 27–29 MD	61	91
2	**32:** 16–20 MC	62	92
3	33	63	93
4	34	64	94
5	35	65	95
6: 20, 23, 91, 93, 114, 141, 151–53 MD	36	66	96
7: 163–170 MD	37	67	97
8	38	**68:** 33, 48–50 MD	98
9	**39:** 52–54 MD	69	99
10: 490, 94–6 MD	**40:** 56–57 MD	70	100
11: 12, 17, 114 MD	41	71	101
12: 1–3, 7 MD	**42:** 23–25, 27 MD	72	102
13	43	**73:** 10–11, 20 MD	103
14: 28–29 MC	44	74	104
15	45	75	105
16	**46:** 10, 15, 35 MD	76	106
17: 26, 32–3, 57, 73–80 MD	**47:** 13 MC	77	**107:** 4–7 MD
18	48	78	108
19: 58. 71	49	79	109
20: 130–131 MD	50	80	110
21	51	81	112
22: 52–55 MC	52	82	113
23	**53:** 32 MD	**83:** 281 MC	114
24	**54:** 44–46 MD	84	
25: 68–70 MD	55	85	
26: 97, 224–227 MD	**56:** 81–82 MD	86	
27	57	87	
28: 52–55, 85 MD	58	88	
29: 1–11 MC	59	89	
30: 17 MC	60	90	
MD = verses revealed at Medina; MC = verses revealed at Mecca			

References

Afkhami, Mahnaz. 1995. *Faith and Freedom: Women's Human Rights in the Muslim World*. London: I. B. Tauris.

Ahmed, Leila. 1992. *Women and Gender in Islam: Historical Roots of a Modern Debate*. New Haven: Yale University Press.

Ali, Abdullah Yusuf. 2001. *The Meaning of the Holy Qur'an*. 10th edn. Beltsville, MD: Amana. Online at www.islam101.com/quran/yusufAli/

Arabic Gospel of the Infancy. Translated by Alexander Roberts and James Donaldson. Online at http://wesley.nnu.edu/Biblical_Studies/noncanon/gospels/infarab.htm

Arberry, A. J. 1955. *The Koran Interpreted*. London: Allen & Unwin. Online at http://arthursclassicnovels.com/arthurs/koran/koran-arberry10.html

Barlas, Asma. 2006. "Women's Readings of the Qur'an", in Jane Dammen McAuliffe (ed.), *The Cambridge Companion to the Qur'an*. Cambridge: Cambridge University Press, 255–71.

Al-Bukhari. 1987. *The Translation of the Meaning of Sahih Al-Bukhari*. Translated by M. M. Khan. New Delhi: Kitab Bhavan. (References are to book and hadith numbers.)

Cragg, Kenneth. 1994. *The Event of the Qur'ān: Islam in its Scripture*. 2nd edn. Oxford: Oneworld.

Cragg, Kenneth. 2005. *The Qur'an and the West*. Washington, DC: Georgetown University Press.

Crone, Patricia, and M. A. Cook. 1977. *Hagarism: The Making of the Islamic World*. Cambridge: Cambridge University Press.

Dawood, N. J. 2000. *The Koran: With a Parallel Arabic Text*. Penguin Classics. London: Penguin Books.

Denffer, Ahmad Von. 1994. *'Ulum al-Qur'an: An Introduction to the Sciences of the Qur'an*. Rev. edn. Leicester: Islamic Foundation.

Donner, Fred. 2006. "The Historical Context", in Jane Dammen McAullife (ed.), *Cambridge Companion to the Qur'an*. Cambridge: Cambridge University Press, 23–39.

Drummond, Richard Henry. 2005. *Islam for the Western Mind: Understanding Muhammad and the Koran*. Charlottesville, VA: Hampton Roads.

Esack, Farid. 1997. *Qur'an, Liberation and Pluralism: An Islamic Perspective of Interreligious Solidarity against Oppression*. Oxford: Oneworld.

Esack, Farid. 2005. *The Qur'an: A User's Guide*. Oxford: Oneworld.

Firestone, Reuven. 1999. *Jihād: The Origin of Holy War in Islam*. New York: Oxford University Press.

Fischer, Michael M. J. and Abedi, Mehdi. 1990. *Debating Muslims: Current Dialogues in Postmodernity and Tradition*. Madison, WI: University of Wisconsin Press.

Ghazālī, Muḥammad, and A. A. Shamis. 2000. *A Thematic Commentary on the Qur'an*. 3 vols. Herndon, VA: International Institute of Islamic Thought.

Gilliot, Claude. 2006. "Creation of a Fixed Text", in Jane Dammen McAuliffe (ed.), *Cambridge Companion to the Qur'an*. Cambridge: Cambridge University Press, 41–57.

Glassé, Cyril. 2008. *The New Encyclopedia of Islam*. Lanham, MD: Rowman & Littlefield.

Graham, William and Navid Kermani. 2006. "Recitation and Aesthetic Reception", in Jane Dammen McAullife (ed.), *Cambridge Companion to the Qur'an*. Cambridge: Cambridge University Press, 115–41.

Guillaume, Alfred. 1996. *The Life of Muhammad: A Translation of Isḥāq's Sīrat rasūl Allāh*. Karachi: Oxford University Press.

Haleem, Muhammad Abdel. 1999. *Understanding The Qur'an: Themes and Style*. London: I. B. Tauris.

Hughes, Thomas Patrick. 1995. *A Dictionary of Islam: Being a Cyclopaedia of the Doctrines, Rites, Ceremonies, and Customs, together with the Technical and Theological Terms, of the Muhammadan Religion*. New Delhi: Asian Educational Services.

Ibn Ishaq. 1966. *The Life of Muhammad: A Translation of Isḥāq's Sīrat rasūl Allāh*. Translated by Alfred Guillaume. Karachi: Oxford University Press. The original translation was 1955.

Jones, Alan. 2001. "Introduction", in J. M. Rodwell, *The Koran*. London: Phoenix, xi–xxvii

Ibn Kathir. 2000. *Tafsir Ibn Kathir*. 10 vols. Abridged. Riyadh: Darussalam.

Kepel, Gilles. 2006. *Jihad: The Trail of Political Islam*. 4th edn. Cambridge, MA: Harvard University Press.

Kabbani, Rana. 1989. *A Letter to Christendom*. London: Virago.

Khan, Muhammad Muhsin. 1987. *The Translation of the Meaning of Sahih al-Bukhari*. Atabic–English. Rev. edn. New Delhi: Kitab Bhavan. Online at www.usc.edu/dept/MSA/fundamentals/hadithsunnah/bukhari

Lawrence, Bruce. 2006. *The Qur'an: A Biography*. New York: Atlantic Monthly Press.

Leaman, Oliver. 2006. *The Qur'an: An Encyclopedia*. London: Routledge.

Leemhuis, Fred. 2006. "From Palm Leaves to the Internet", in Jane Dammen McAullife (ed.), *Cambridge Companion to the Qur'an*. Cambridge: Cambridge University Press, 145–61.

Lings, Martin. 1983. *Muhammad: His Life based on the Earliest Sources*. Rochester, VM: Inner Traditions International.

Madigan, Daniel A. 2006. "Themes and Topics", in Jane Dammen McAullife (ed.), *Cambridge Companion to the Qur'an*. Cambridge: Cambridge University Press, 79–95.

Masood, Steven. 2001. *The Bible and the Qur'an: A Question of Integrity*, Carlisle: OM

McAuliffe, Jane Dammen. 2006. "The Tasks and Traditions of Interpretation", in Jane Dammen McAullife (ed.), *Cambridge Companion to the Qur'an*. Cambridge: Cambridge University Press, 181–209.

Mernissi, Fatima. 1991. *The Veil and the Male Elite: A Feminist Interpretation of Women's Rights in Islam*. Reading, MA: Addison-Wesley.

Muir, William. 1912, 2005. *The Life of Mohammad from Original Sources*. Edinburgh: John Grant; Boston: Adamant Media.

Nasr, Seyyed Hossein. 1987. *Islamic Art and Spirituality*. Albany: State University of New York Press.

Neuwirth, Angelika. 2006. "Structural, Linguistic and Literary Features", in Jane Dammen McAullife (ed.), *Cambridge Companion to the Qur'an*. Cambridge: Cambridge University Press, 97–113.

Nöldeke, Theodor, Friedrich Schwally and Gotthelf Bergsträsser. 1961. *Geschichte des Qorāns*. Hildesheim: Olms.

Parrinder, Edward Geoffrey. 1995. *Jesus in the Qur'ān*. Oxford: Oneworld.

Parsons, Martin. 2005. *Unveiling God: Contextualizing Christology for Islamic Culture*. Pasadena, CA: William Carey Library.

Pickthall, Muhammad Marmaduke. 1977. *The Meaning of the Glorious Qur'an: Text and Explanatory Translation*. Mecca: Muslim World League. Online at www.islam101.com/quran/QTP/index.htm.

Qutb, Sayyid, M. A. Salahi and Ashur A. Shamis. 2002. *In the Shade of the Quran = Fi Zilal al-Quran*. Markfield: Islamic Foundation. Online at http://islamworld.net/docs/qutb/shade.html

Reeves, Minou. 2003. *Muhammad In Europe*. New York: New York University Press.

Rippin, Andrew, and Jan Knappert. 1990. *Textual Sources for the Study of Islam*. Chicago: University of Chicago Press.

Robinson, Neal. 2003. *Discovering the Qur'an: A Contemporary Approach to a Veiled Text*. 2nd edn. London: SCM Press.

Rodwell, J. M. 2001. *The Koran*. London: Phoenix. Online at www.truthnet.org/islam/Quran/Rodwell/

Saeed, Abdullah. 2006. *Interpreting the Qur'ān towards a Contemporary Approach*. Abingdon: Routledge.

Saeed, Abdullah. 2008. *The Qur'an: An Introduction*. London: Routledge.

Sahas, Daniel J. 1972. *John of Damascus on Islam*. Leiden: Brill.

Sarwar, Muhammad and Bernard Toropov. 2003. *The Complete Idiot's Guide to the Koran*. Indianapolis, IN: Alpha.

Sells, Michael. 2007. *Approaching the Qur'an: The Early Revelations*. 2nd edn. Ashland, OR: White Cloud Press.

Sherif, Faruq. 1995. *A Guide to the Contents of the Qur'an*. Reading: Garnet.

Sonn, Tamara. 2002. 'Muslims in South Africa: A Very Visible Minority', in Yvonne Yazbeck Haddad and Jane I. Smith (eds), *Muslim Minorities in the West: Visible and Invisible*. Walnut Creek, CA: AltaMira Press, 144–55.

Spencer, Robert. 2006. *The Truth about Muhammad: Founder of the World's Most Intolerant Religion*. Washington, DC: Regnery.

Sultan, Sohaib. 2004. *The Koran for Dummies*. Hoboken, NJ: Wiley.

Sultan, Sohaib. 2007. *The Qur'an and Sayings of Prophet Muhammad: Selections Annotated and Explained*. Woodstock, VT: SkyLight Paths.

Taha, Mahmud Muhammad. 1987. *The Second Message of Islam*. Translated by Abdullahi Ahmed an-Na'im. Syracuse, NY: Syracuse University Press.

Wadud, Amina. 1999. *Qur'an and Woman: Rereading the Sacred Text from a Woman's Perspective*. New York: Oxford University Press.

Wansbrough, John E. 1977, 2004. *Quranic Studies: Sources and Methods of Scriptural Interpretation*. London Oriental Series 31. Oxford: Oxford University Press; Amherst, NY: Prometheus.

Weil, Gustav. 1843. *Mohammed der Prophet, sein Leben und seine Lehre: aus handschriftlichen Quellen und dem Koran geschöpft und dargestellt*. Stuttgart: Metzler'schen Buchhandlung.

Zaid, Nasr Hamid Abu. 1998. "Divine Attributes in the Qur'an: Some Poetic Aspects", in John Cooper, Ronald Nettler and Mohamed Mahmoud (eds), *Islam and Modernity: Muslim Intellectuals Respond*, London, I. B. Tauris, 190–211.

Zakaria, Rafiq. 1991. *Muhammad and the Quran*. New Delhi: Penguin Books.

Qur'anic Index

Index to Verses referenced (excluding within paraphrases).

Index of Bible References